ClearRevise®

OCR GCSE
Business J204

Illustrated revision and practice

Published by
PG Online Limited
The Old Coach House
35 Main Road
Tolpuddle
Dorset
DT2 7EW
United Kingdom

sales@pgonline.co.uk
www.clearrevise.com
www.pgonline.co.uk
2024

PG ONLINE

PREFACE

Absolute clarity! That's the aim.

This is everything you need to ace the examined component in this course and beam with pride. Each topic is laid out in a beautifully illustrated format that is clear, approachable and as concise and simple as possible.

Each section of the specification is clearly indicated to help you cross-reference your revision. The checklist on the contents pages will help you keep track of what you have already worked through and what's left before the big day.

We have included worked exam-style questions with answers for almost every topic. This helps you understand where marks are coming from and to see the theory at work for yourself in an exam situation. There is also a set of exam-style questions at the end of each section for you to practise writing answers for. You can check your answers against those given at the end of the book.

LEVELS OF LEARNING

Based on the degree to which you are able to truly understand a new topic, we recommend that you work in stages. Start by reading a short explanation of something, then try and recall what you've just read. This has limited effect if you stop there but it aids the next stage. Question everything. Write down your own summary and then complete and mark a related exam-style question. Cover up the answers if necessary but learn from them once you've seen them. Lastly, teach someone else. Explain the topic in a way that they can understand. Have a go at the different practice questions – they offer an insight into how and where marks are awarded.

ACKNOWLEDGMENTS

Every effort has been made to trace and acknowledge ownership of copyright. The publishers will be happy to make any future amendments with copyright owners that it has not been possible to contact. The publisher would like to thank the following companies and individuals who granted permission for the use of their images in this textbook.

Design and artwork: Jessica Webb / PG Online Ltd
Photographic images: © Shutterstock
Play-Doh image © Ekaterina_Minaeva / Shutterstock.com

First edition 2024   10 9 8 7 6 5 4 3 2 1
A catalogue entry for this book is available from the British Library
ISBN: 978-1-916518-12-4
Contributor: Paul Clark
Copyright © PG Online 2024
All rights reserved
No part of this publication may be reproduced, stored in a retrieval system, or transmitted in any form or by any means without the prior written permission of the copyright owner.
This product is made of material from well-managed FSC®-certified forests and from recycled materials.
Printed by Bell & Bain Ltd, Glasgow, UK.

THE SCIENCE OF REVISION

Illustrations and words

Research has shown that revising with words and pictures doubles the quality of responses by students.[1] This is known as 'dual-coding' because it provides two ways of fetching the information from our brain. The improvement in responses is particularly apparent in students when they are asked to apply their knowledge to different problems. Recall, application and judgement are all specifically and carefully assessed in public examination questions.

Retrieval of information

Retrieval practice encourages students to come up with answers to questions.[2] The closer the question is to one you might see in a real examination, the better. Also, the closer the environment in which a student revises is to the 'examination environment', the better. Students who had a test 2–7 days away did 30% better using retrieval practice than students who simply read, or repeatedly reread material. Students who were expected to teach the content to someone else after their revision period did better still.[3] What was found to be most interesting in other studies is that students using retrieval methods and testing for revision were also more resilient to the introduction of stress.[4]

Ebbinghaus' forgetting curve and spaced learning

Ebbinghaus' 140-year-old study examined the rate at which we forget things over time. The findings still hold true. However, the act of forgetting facts and techniques and relearning them is what cements them into the brain.[6] Spacing out revision is more effective than cramming – we know that, but students should also know that the space between revisiting material should vary depending on how far away the examination is. A cyclical approach is required. An examination 12 months away necessitates revisiting covered material about once a month. A test in 30 days should have topics revisited every 3 days – intervals of roughly a tenth of the time available.[6]

Summary

Students: the more tests and past questions you do, in an environment as close to examination conditions as possible, the better you are likely to perform on the day. If you prefer to listen to music while you revise, tunes without lyrics will be far less detrimental to your memory and retention. Silence is most effective.[5] If you choose to study with friends, choose carefully – effort is contagious.[7]

---

1. Mayer, R. E., & Anderson, R. B. (1991). Animations need narrations: An experimental test of dual-coding hypothesis. *Journal of Education Psychology*, (83)4, 484–490.
2. Roediger III, H. L., & Karpicke, J.D. (2006). Test-enhanced learning: Taking memory tests improves long-term retention. *Psychological Science*, 17(3), 249–255.
3. Nestojko, J., Bui, D., Kornell, N. & Bjork, E. (2014). Expecting to teach enhances learning and organisation of knowledge in free recall of text passages. *Memory and Cognition*, 42(7), 1038–1048.
4. Smith, A. M., Floerke, V. A., & Thomas, A. K. (2016) Retrieval practice protects memory against acute stress. *Science*, 354(6315), 1046–1048.
5. Perham, N., & Currie, H. (2014). Does listening to preferred music improve comprehension performance? *Applied Cognitive Psychology*, 28(2), 279–284.
6. Cepeda, N. J., Vul, E., Rohrer, D., Wixted, J. T. & Pashler, H. (2008). Spacing effects in learning a temporal ridgeline of optimal retention. *Psychological Science*, 19(11), 1095–1102.
7. Busch, B. & Watson, E. (2019), *The Science of Learning*, 1st ed. Routledge.

CONTENTS

Questions and marking

Mark allocations vi
Command words vii

Paper 1: Business activity, marketing and people

Section 1

Specification point

1.1	Business enterprise and entrepreneurship	2
1.2	Business planning	4
1.3	Business ownership	6
1.3	Liability	8
1.4	Business aims and objectives	10
1.5	Stakeholders in business	12
1.6	Business growth	14
	Case study	16
	Examination practice	**17**

Section 2

2.1	The role of marketing	18
2.2	Primary market research methods	20
2.2	Secondary market research	21
2.2	Appropriateness of research	22
2.2	Use and interpretation of data	23
2.3	Market segmentation	24
2.4	Marketing mix: Product	25
2.4	Product life cycle	26
2.4	The marketing mix: Price	27
2.4	The marketing mix: Promotion	28
2.4	The marketing mix: Place	30
2.4	The marketing mix	32
2.4	Interpretation of market data	34
	Case study	36
	Examination practice	**37**

iv ClearRevise

Section 3

3.1	The role of human resources	38
3.2	Organisational structure	39
3.3	Communication in business	42
3.4	Recruitment and selection	44
3.5	Motivation and retention	46
3.6	Training and development	48
3.6	Staff development	50
3.7	Employment law	51
	Case study	*52*
	Examination practice	**53**

Paper 2: Operations, finance and influences on business

Section 4

4.1	Production processes	55
4.1	Influence of technology on production	56
4.2	The concept of quality	57
4.2	The importance of quality	58
4.3	Methods of selling	59
4.3	Customer service	60
4.4	Consumer law	62
4.5	Business location	63
4.6	Working with suppliers	64
	Case study	*66*
	Examination practice	**67**

Section 5

5.1	The finance function	68
5.2	Why businesses need finance	69
5.2	Source of finance	70
5.3	Revenue, costs, profit and loss	72
5.3	Average rate of return	74
5.4	Break-even	76
5.5	Cash-flow	78
	Case study	*80*
	Examination practice	**81**

Section 6

6.1	Ethical and environmental considerations	82
6.2	The economic climate	84
6.3	Globalisation	86
	Case study	*88*
	Examination practice	**89**

Section 7

7	The interdependent nature of business	90
	Case study	*92*
	Examination practice	**93**

Examination practice answers	94
Formulae	100
Index	101
Examination tips	**103**

MARK ALLOCATIONS

Green mark allocations *[1]* on answers to in-text questions throughout this guide help to indicate where marks are gained within the answers. A bracketed '1' e.g. *[1]* = one valid point worthy of a mark. In longer answer questions, a mark is given based on the whole response. In these answers, the following marks indicate how marks are awarded. There are often many more points to make than there are marks available so you have more opportunity to max out your answers than you may think.

[K] indicates where a mark is gained for demonstrating **knowledge**. (AO1a)

[U] indicates where **understanding** has been demonstrated. (AO1b)

[APP] indicates where a mark is gained for **application** of knowledge. (AO2)

[AN] indicates where a mark is gained through **analysis**, covering Assessment Objective 3a (AO3a).

[EVAL] indicates where a mark is gained through the use of **evaluation**. (AO3b)

COMMAND WORDS

Multiple choice questions

Both Paper 1 and Paper 2 start with a series of 15 multiple choice questions. Each question has a space for you to write the letter (A, B, C or D) of your choice.

Identify or state

You may be asked to 'identify two....' or to 'State,....' If this is the case, then you only have to demonstrate knowledge. You do not need to develop your answers.

Calculate

Calculation questions will be worth 2-3 marks, depending on the number of steps you need to do to get to the final answer. You do not get any marks for simply writing the formula unless the question specifically states this. A correct answer will always score full marks, but ensure you show your working out. If your answer is incorrect, you may get some marks for correct workings. If the question asks for 1 or 2 decimal places, make sure you reflect this in your answer, or you will lose a mark.

Explain

There are four types of 'Explain' questions. They will be either worth 2 or 4 marks.

- The first is a non-contextualised 2-mark Explain question. This type of question will be generic and not linked to a particular business. For this, you will have to make a valid point and then have one relevant linked strand of development. To do this, you need to use clear connectives such as *'therefore'*, *'this leads to'*, *'because'*, *'so'* and *'as a result'*. Try to avoid the use of the word 'also' as this indicates you are moving onto a second point.

- The second is a 2-mark contextualised Explain question. These questions will follow on from a case study. You need to do everything as mentioned for the first type but now also need to make your answer specific about the particular business in the question.

- The third type is worth 4 marks. These will ask you to 'Explain two....'. This means that you need to do everything for the 2-mark contextualised Explain question twice.

- The final type is simply a variation on a theme. It will be worth 6 marks and will ask you to 'Explain three......' Therefore, you have to make three points. Each point must contain application and a linked strand of logical development.

Analyse

Analyse questions will always be worth 3 marks. There are three assessment objectives covered in these questions. You have to demonstrate knowledge by providing a valid benefit, drawback or impact (or whatever it is you are asked to analyse). You then have to give two linked strands of logical development, one of which must be contextualised to the case study or question to showcase your skills of application. The other will be awarded an analysis mark.

Recommend

This will be the third subsection of a chain of questions. Previously you may have been asked to analyse the advantage and disadvantage of something (or it could be that you have had to analyse two different options). This third part will then ask you to recommend which is the stronger argument or best course of action to take. You must make a decision and explain why you have made that decision in the context of the business presented in the case study.

Evaluate and Discuss

These questions can be worth between 7 and 9 marks and examine all four skill areas:

- Knowledge and understanding
- Application
- Analysis
- Evaluation

To score highly in these questions, you must demonstrate that you can weigh up both sides of an argument or be able to compare alternatives. It's best to address both sides, applying your answers to the case study and showing linked strands of logical development. You are required to conclude your answer. Which argument is stronger and why? Why might a particular course of action be best for a business to take?

TOPICS FOR PAPER 1
Business activity, marketing and people

Information about the paper

Specification coverage
Business activity, marketing and people

Assessment
Written exam: 1 hour 30 minutes
80 marks
All questions are mandatory
50% of the qualification grade
Calculators are permitted in this examination.

Assessment overview
The paper is divided into two sections:
Section A: 15 marks
Section B: 65 marks
Section A consists of 15 multiple choice questions. Questions in Section B will be based on business contexts given in the paper.
The paper will consist of calculations, multiple-choice, short-answer and extended-writing questions.

1.1

BUSINESS ENTERPRISE AND ENTREPRENEURSHIP

An **enterprise** is a business that has the ability to identify a business idea and can take a risk in seeing that the idea is brought to market. A business owner is someone who starts and runs their own business. An **entrepreneur** generally takes on higher risk in introducing newer ideas into a market. In doing so, the entrepreneur needs to demonstrate the necessary skills to be successful.

Purpose of business enterprise and entrepreneurship

- Spotting a business opportunity
- Developing an idea for a business
- Satisfying the needs of customers

Explain **one** purpose of business enterprise and entrepreneurship. [2]

One purpose is to satisfy the needs of customers.[1] An entrepreneur can do this by adapting products to meet the individual needs of customers.[1]

Explain questions are worth 2 marks and may or may not be linked to a case study. You are required you to give a valid point, with one linked strand of development.

Characteristics of an entrepreneur

The following are the skills or abilities that a successful entrepreneur will possess:

Creativity: An entrepreneur needs to come up with new ideas and inventive ways to alter a product in order to continue to meet consumer needs. Being creative also incorporates coming up with better ways of producing a product or providing a service.

Risk-taking: Running a business venture is risky, but to be successful an entrepreneur must be able to acknowledge and evaluate these risks. Risks can be managed, and steps can be taken to reduce them, but an entrepreneur cannot plan for every eventuality and must be prepared to accept the outcomes of their actions and decisions.

Determination: There will be times when things don't go to plan or difficulties arise. A successful entrepreneur will not let this put them off and will show resilience to overcome the problems that they face.

Confidence: An entrepreneur must believe in their own ability and back themselves to succeed.

Risk and reward

When deciding whether to go ahead with a business venture, or when making business decisions, an entrepreneur will have to consider the risks and rewards associated with it. Some businesses may be deemed to be riskier than others. Common examples of such businesses are those that face seasonal demand or operate in highly competitive markets.

Risk

Business failure
The ultimate risk that an entrepreneur faces when starting a business is failure. A lot of businesses will fail because they will run out of funds and therefore cannot afford to pay for everything they need to.

Financial loss
Businesses risk losing the capital investment that the owner has put into the business if the business were to fail. If the business has unlimited liability this could mean that the owner's personal belongings could be at risk if the business cannot afford to pay all its debts.

Lack of security
When an individual sets up a business, they do not have a guaranteed regular income. They will also not benefit from sick, holiday or maternity pay. This could make paying their own bills, such as a mortgage, very difficult with severe consequences for missing payments.

Reward

Profit
A business will make a profit when its revenue exceeds its total costs over a period of time. This would be the financial reward that most entrepreneurs will seek in return for the risks they take.

Independence
Many entrepreneurs will value working for themselves and benefiting from the freedoms that this may bring, rather than working for someone else who may dictate their working hours. Independence allows the entrepreneur to make all the key decisions which can be very rewarding.

Self-satisfaction
Many entrepreneurs seek the feel-good factor that comes with running a successful business. This feeling can also be achieved by an entrepreneur who sets a social objective of improving the lives of others in some way.

1.2

BUSINESS PLANNING

A **business plan** is a working document that details the objectives that a business wants to achieve and how it will set about achieving them. It looks at all aspects of the business so that risk is reduced, giving the business a greater chance to succeed.

Purpose of business planning activity

The main purpose of creating a business plan is to **reduce the risk** that the entrepreneur faces in setting up a business. In doing so, it will **help the business to succeed**. Business planning helps an entrepreneur to think ahead and assess the difficulties that they may face, allowing them to make better informed decisions. There will always be the chance that something unforeseen could happen which could negatively impact a business. However, through producing a business plan, an entrepreneur will be thinking about a lot of different scenarios and considering how the business could deal with each of them.

The role, importance and usefulness of a business plan

To identify markets: A business plan will allow an entrepreneur to establish their target demographic market, often through carrying out detailed market research. Through planning, they will also know which geographical markets to target, or whether they should locate online.

A demographic market is a section of the population with similar characteristics, for example teenagers or vegetarians.

A geographic market is the place in which a product may be offered for sale.

To help obtain finance Any potential investor will want to know that their investment is as secure as possible. Although risk cannot be eliminated, a business plan can reassure potential investors that income and costs have been considered.

To identify the resources a business needs to operate: An entrepreneur will know what physical resources (materials) are needed to produce the goods or provide the service. They will also know what human resources (people) they require. Through business planning, an entrepreneur can ensure each functional area (Marketing, Operations, HR and Finance) is sufficiently resourced.

To set and achieve aims and objectives: A business plan will detail what the business hopes to achieve and how. By monitoring progress against these objectives, entrepreneurs can make appropriate decisions to help meet their targets.

Example

A business plan needs to consider all aspects of the business, including some background information on the entrepreneur and details of their idea. Each of the functions will also be considered.

Details of the entrepreneur:
- Experience and skills of the entrepreneur(s).

Financial forecasts:
- Budgets of income and expenditure.
- Cash-flow forecasts.
- Break-even analysis.

Marketing plan:
- Market research to be carried out.
- Details of the target market.
- Details of the marketing mix.
- Details of the competitors and how the business will compete.

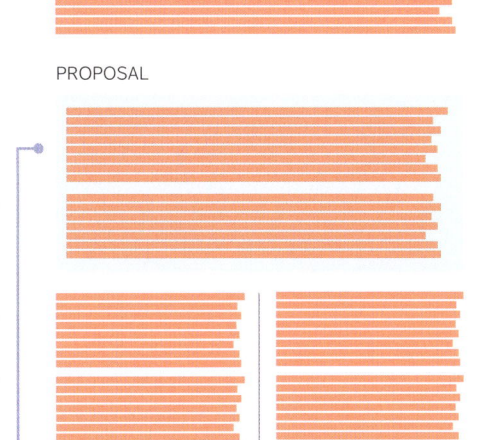

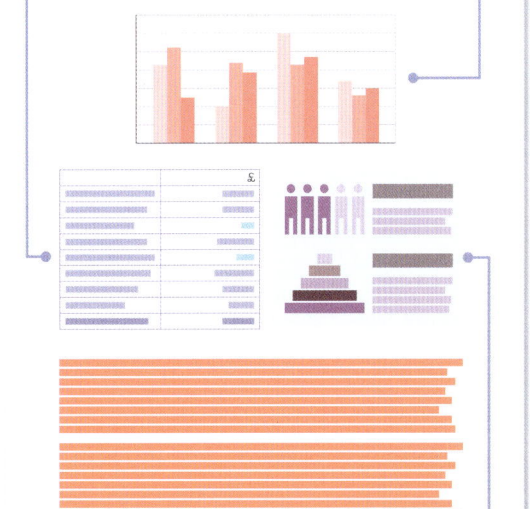

The business idea:
- Details of proposed business activity
- The business' aims and objectives.
- The legal structure of the business.
- How the business is to be financed.

Resources required:
- Details of supplies needed and the suppliers the business will use.
- The equipment and machinery that is necessary.

Staff required:
- The number of employees needed and the skill sets that they must possess.
- How the business is to be structured including job roles and pay structures.

OCR GCSE **Business**

1.3

BUSINESS OWNERSHIP

When an entrepreneur decides to start up a business, they have a number of different options for its formation. Each option will have an impact on the legal status of the business.

The features of different types of business ownership

Sole trader

A **sole trader** is a business that is owned and operated by one person.

Benefits	Drawbacks	Suitability
• Quick and easy to set up. • Sole trader keeps all the profits. • Sole trader controls all the decisions. • Business' financial information is kept private.	• Sole trader faces unlimited liability. See **page 8**. • Finance may be limited to own funding. / May be more difficult to raise further finance. • Business may not run if sole trader is off sick or takes a holiday. • Heavy workload. • Need to possess a wide range of skills. • Need to work long hours.	Common for start-up businesses, because: • They often require a small amount of finance. • It is the simplest form of business to set up and start trading with. • They are often a low financial risk.

Partnership

A **partnership** is an unincorporated business which has two or more owners who share the risk.

Benefits	Drawbacks	Suitability
• Each partner could contribute finance. • Each partner can bring ideas and different skills. • The workload can be shared. • Business' financial information is kept private. • Control is shared between partners.	• Partners face unlimited liability. • There may be disagreements between the partners. • Profits have to be shared amongst partners according to agreed ratios	Used by a start-up or established business, when: • More finance is needed. • A broader range of skills is required. • There is a fairly low level of financial risk. • Owners want to share the risk and workload.

6 Clear**Revise**

The features of different types of business ownership continued

Agreements between partners

Partners draw up an agreement explaining how their partnership will work. It will include the following details:

- How **profits** are to be shared.
- The **salary** levels of the partners.
- The percentage **voting rights** of each partner.
- How the **workload** is to be shared.
- The level of **investment** by each partner.
- The **sharing of liability**.
- The **decision-making** process (and decision-making powers of each partner).

Bohdan is a Ukrainian chef residing in the UK. He has embarked on a new venture after completing a catering course by launching an outside catering business specialising in exquisite Eastern European cuisine for private functions. Despite having a popular concept, Bohdan faces a financial hurdle as he lacks the funds necessary to purchase essential cookery equipment. He is also worried that he won't be able to cater for many people on his own. His friend Giles, also a trained chef looking for work, has savings of £15,000 – sufficient to cover the cost of the equipment. Recognising a mutually beneficial opportunity, Bohdan proposed a partnership with Giles, combining their culinary expertise and resources to establish and grow their unique catering business.

Analyse **one** benefit to Bohdan of setting up in partnership with Giles. [3]

Bohdan will be able to gain a higher investment into the business.[1] This is because Giles has £15,000 worth of savings.[1] Therefore the business will be more able to purchase the cookery equipment needed.[1]

Bohdan will be able to take on more work for larger private functions[1] since he now has another chef to help share the workload.[1] This will increase their revenue / so that they are able to repay the cost of equipment sooner.[1]

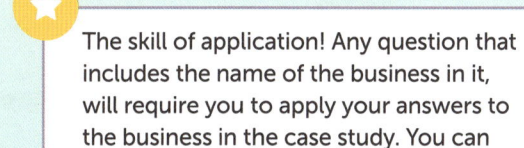

The skill of application! Any question that includes the name of the business in it, will require you to apply your answers to the business in the case study. You can do this by using evidence from the text.

In the example **above**, the answers use the fact that Giles has £15,000 in savings or that Bohdan wants to cater for larger private functions. This is the evidence needed from the case study to gain the mark for application.

1.3

LIABILITY

Liability refers to the responsibility of the owners for a business' debts. **Unincorporated** businesses (sole traders and partnerships) will have **unlimited liability**, whereas a company's liability will be limited.

Unlimited liability

If a business owner has **unlimited liability**, they and the business are seen as the same legal entity. This is known as **unincorporated**. Any debts that the business has will be the total responsibility of the owner. If the business cannot pay the debts off, then the owner may have to sell personal possessions to clear them.

Limited liability

If a business owner has **limited liability**, they are seen as separate from the business in the eyes of the law. This is called incorporation. Therefore, the debts of the business are not regarded as personal debts of the owner, so their personal possessions are protected and there is a guaranteed limit to their losses. The owner is only liable for the amount of money that they have invested.

Sole traders and partnerships typically have unlimited liability.

What does limited liability mean for business owners? [1]
- A: Owners are not responsible for any business debts.
- B: Owners are only responsible for any business debts up to the amount they invested.
- C: Owners are personally responsible for all business debts.
- D: Owners can claim business losses back from the government.

B Owners are only responsible for any business debts up to the amount they invested. [1]

Companies

Private limited companies (ltd)

This is an incorporated business which is owned by shareholders. Shares can only be sold privately, with the permission of the other existing shareholders, usually to friends and family.

Benefits	Drawbacks	Suitability
- Easier to raise finance by selling shares. - Owners have **limited liability**. The business is responsible for paying its debts. - Directors are often also shareholders and can benefit from dividend payments.	- Overall control could be lost. - The company's accounts and financial information is made public. - More legal paperwork involved when setting up as it is more complex. - Potential for disagreement between directors and shareholders.	It can be suitable for start-ups but also established businesses wanting to grow when: - More finance is needed. - Owners seek financial protection because risk is increased. - Owners wish to keep control of the business.

Public limited companies (plc)

A PLC is an incorporated business that can access huge financial resources by selling shares on a stock exchange. This is achieved through **flotation**. A public limited company is controlled and managed by a Board of Directors who are voted into the position by shareholders at an **Annual General Meeting** (**AGM**).

Benefits	Drawbacks	Suitability
- Can raise large amounts of finance by selling shares to the general public. - Shareholders have **limited liability**. - Public are more aware of the business and perceive them as more reliable.	- At risk from potential takeovers. - Potential loss of control, for original owners, after flotation. - There will be increased media scrutiny into their activities. - More detailed financial reports and accounts are available for public viewing.	Suitable for established businesses that: - Need large amounts of additional finance. - Want to grow. - Have a high financial risk. - Have owners that don't mind losing control.

OCR GCSE **Business**

1.4

BUSINESS AIMS AND OBJECTIVES

An **aim** is what a business hopes to achieve in the long term. It can also be referred to as the goal of a business; it is the reason that the business is in existence. An **objective** is more specific and is the short-term target that a business seeks in order to fulfil their aim.

The aims and objectives of business

Survival – Businesses must bring in enough cash to pay for all their bills so that they can continue to trade. Sufficient **cash flow** is crucial to survival.

Profit maximisation – Business revenue that exceeds its costs creates profit. This is the main objective for many businesses, particularly those in the private sector. This can be achieved by focusing on growth or on lowering costs.

Growth – A well-established business that is financially successful may decide to grow, either domestically or by expanding operations overseas.

Providing a service – Businesses may seek to improve their customer satisfaction rating. This is done by improving the level of customer service or by increasing the range of products available.

Market share – This is the percentage of the total sales in a market made by one business. Sometimes a business will prioritise increasing their market share so that they can become the dominant firm.

How and why objectives might change as businesses evolve

As businesses grow, what they aim to achieve may need adapting. A well-established firm that is experiencing high demand may no longer need survival as its main objective, but instead may aim for growth. Many factors affect the aims and objectives that a business will pursue.

Market conditions – The level of economic activity will impact a business' aim. When consumers have lots of disposable income and demand is high, a business may have new opportunities to seek growth.

Technology – A business' aim may have to change due to changes in technology. Technology may allow for new and improved inventions to be designed and manufactured. Spending money in innovation may be more important than growth, particularly if competitors are taking advantage of it.

Legislation – New regulation may impact the aims and objectives of a business as it may affect the products and services that the business offers or those that it can import and export.

Internal reasons – New owners or managers may have a different vision for the business. A change in technology or financial stability may no longer support initial plans. Staffing situations may change which affect what is possible to achieve in a given time frame.

1. Explain **one** reason why a business might set objectives. [2]

   1. To provide a target,[1] therefore the business' performance by comparison can be judged and necessary action taken.[1] To provide direction / to motivate employees,[1] because they all understand the common goal they are working towards.[1]

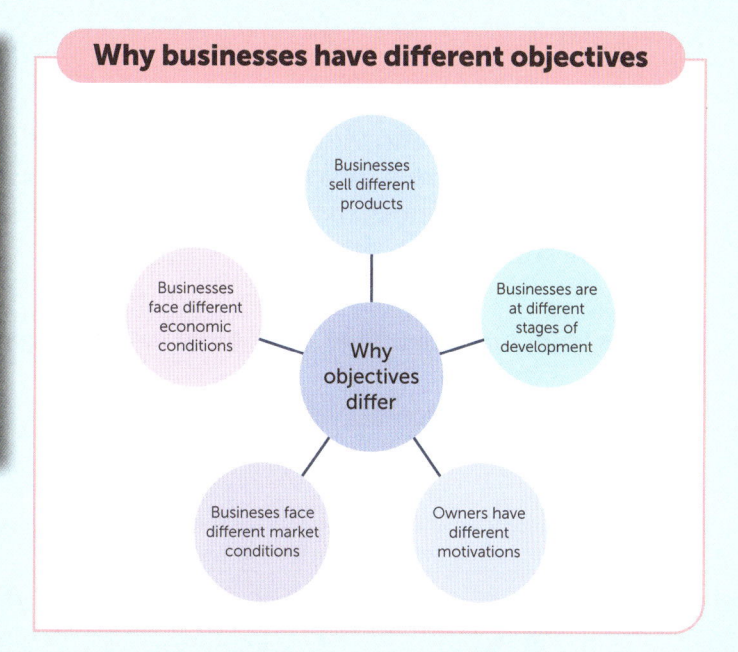

Why businesses have different objectives

- Businesses sell different products
- Businesses are at different stages of development
- Owners have different motivations
- Businesses face different market conditions
- Businesses face different economic conditions

Why objectives differ

2. Sarah-Jayne, founder of Rose Bees gardening business, experienced rapid initial success, quickly attracting a substantial customer base. After a successful first year, she decided to expand, investing in additional equipment, hiring two employees and ramping up her marketing efforts. However, the market soon became fiercely competitive with the emergence of many new firms. Increased competition, combined with her rising operational costs, led to dwindling cash reserves as her outgoings surpassed her income. Realising her expenses were unsustainable, Sarah-Jayne faced the challenge of adjusting her business strategy to maintain profitability.

   Analyse **one** reason why Sarah-Jayne may have to change her objective from growth to survival. [3]

   2. One reason is that Sarah-Jayne is running out of cash.[1] This is because the gardening market has become much more competitive.[1] Therefore she is not gaining enough work to keep the two workers she hired occupied.[1]

1.5

STAKEHOLDERS IN BUSINESS

A **stakeholder** is an individual or group that has an interest in a business. Each stakeholder will have a different objective and is affected in different ways by the decisions a business makes. The interests of each stakeholder often come into conflict with each other.

The roles and objectives of internal and external stakeholder groups

Stakeholder	What they want from the business
Internal	
Shareholder (Owner)	Shareholders will commonly want the business to be financially successful so they can maximise the profits or dividends that are made on their investment.
Employees	Workers will want job security and financial reward in return for their effort.
External	
Customers	Customers will want the product or service to fulfil their needs. They will expect good customer service and value for money.
Suppliers	Suppliers will want the business to be successful, so they can continue to receive orders. They will also want to be paid on time.
Local community	Local residents will want the business to be successful, so it continues to offer employment. They will also want the business to do good for their community, both in terms of the environment and in terms of their provision.
Pressure groups	Pressure groups will want businesses to behave in an ethically and environmentally friendly manner. These can include trade unions who may campaign for workers' rights.
The government	The government will want businesses to be successful so that they continue to employ people. Businesses also pay tax to the government.

The effect stakeholders have on businesses

The owners and managers of a business will have a controlling influence on its activity, but they cannot ignore the other stakeholders as they have an influence on how the business operates:
- A business cannot ignore its customers. If they are not listened to, they will purchase products from rivals instead.
- A business needs a happy and motivated workforce so must consider their needs.
- Not paying attention to the needs of suppliers can lead to poor relationships with them.
- Ignoring the wishes of the local community and pressure groups could cause the business to develop a negative reputation.

The effect business activity has on stakeholders

The actions and performance of businesses will impact on all the stakeholders. For instance, if a business were to make a lot of profit, then shareholders will be happier as they will receive higher returns on their investment and may be more likely to commit funds in the future. However, if a manufacturing objective changes shift patterns to start working through the night to increase output, both employees and the local community may not be too happy.

Two biscuit manufacturers have decided to merge in a strategic move to streamline operations and cut costs. As part of the merger, the combined company will reduce the workforce, leading to job losses aimed at decreasing operational expenses. Additionally, they will consolidate their supply chain, opting to use a single major supplier instead of the multiple suppliers they previously relied on. To further enhance efficiency, the merged entity will narrow its product range, focusing on mass-producing one major product line to capitalise on the benefits of large-scale production.

Explain the impact on **two** different stakeholders of the merger between the two businesses. [4]

> *Conflict may exist between owners, who want to make as much profit as possible,[1] and employees, who want to receive higher pay.[1] They may be in conflict as both cannot happen,[1] if employees' pay is increased then costs will also increase, sacrificing profit.[1]*

OCR GCSE **Business**

1.6

BUSINESS GROWTH

After surviving the initial years and becoming established, a business may want to grow. The owners will have to make a decision as to whether they grow organically or externally.

Organic growth

Organic growth is characterised by a business that grows naturally by gradually increasing the number of products that it sells. It is also called **internal growth**. Methods of organic growth are:

Increasing output

A business can grow by simply utilising its resources in a more efficient manner. This could be achieved through using more productive equipment or by training their workers.

Gaining new customers

A business can attract new customers through marketing the product in a different way, e.g. advertising through social media. It can also be done by selling its existing products in new markets. This is achieved by adapting the **marketing mix**, for instance they could aim at a different target market by changing the price or the way a product is promoted. A business could also look to sell its products in new overseas markets, whether that is by physically locating in foreign countries or by using online sales (e-commerce).

Developing new products

Businesses can grow by introducing new products onto the market. Conducting research and development into new ideas, adopting new technology and being innovative will help a business grow.

Increasing market share

Aggressively marketing a product or engaging in marketing tactics to increase sales will increase dominance in a particular market.

---

1. Explain **two** impacts on a business from growing organically. [4]

    1. One impact is that it is slower than growing externally.[1] This could be because you have to convince customers to buy the products which takes time, therefore revenues and sales increase at a slower rate.[1]

       Another impact is that organic growth is cheaper than external growth.[1] This is because the business is growing gradually rather than spending large amounts on purchasing another business.[1]

External growth

External growth happens when a business grows by joining with another business, whether that be by a merger or a takeover. It is also known as **inorganic growth**.

Mergers and takeovers

A **merger** is where two or more businesses agree to join to share resources. A **takeover** is where one business buys a majority shareholding in another.

Some companies increase their product range, either organically or inorganically, in order to spread the risk of one failing to be successful. This is known as diversification.

Benefits of external growth

- Growth can be quicker than internal growth.
- Combined business benefits from shared resources and skills.
- Merging with another similar business can reduce competition.
- Increased market share.

Drawbacks of external growth

- Difficult to integrate two businesses together.
- It can be an expensive process.
- Need to share profits.
- Take on the debts of the other company.

When a merger or takeover occurs, it can be one of three types:

Horizontal integration – This involves a merger or a takeover between two businesses in the same market and at the same stage of production. For example, a chocolate manufacturer merging with another chocolate manufacturer.

Backwards vertical integration – A business merges with, or takes over, another business at an earlier stage of production. For example, a chocolate manufacturer taking over a cocoa farm.

Forwards vertical integration – A business merges with, or takes over, a business at a later stage in production. For example, a chocolate manufacturer buying a retailer.

---

2. A butcher's shop taking over a farm that rears pigs is classified as which type of growth? [1]

   A: Backwards vertical integration
   B: Forwards vertical integration
   C: Horizontal integration
   D: Organic growth

   2. A.[1] This is because the farm is at an earlier stage of the production process.

Topic 1

CASE STUDY

Stabler Gyms is a regional chain of fitness centres, founded by Richard Stabler. Stabler is a fitness enthusiast with a passion for Ironman triathlons and a strong background in the fitness industry. Richard's vision was to create an affordable way for people to stay fit and healthy, leading him to open his first gym. His meticulous business planning and compelling vision enabled him to secure a bank loan to help finance the project, alongside personal savings that he invested. Operating as a limited company for added protection, Richard also brought in his friend Vikram as a shareholder, who contributed financially. This strategic partnership helped Stabler Gyms to not only survive but to thrive in its initial years, growing to eight locations within the region.

Having successfully established a regional presence, Stabler Gyms now aims to expand nationally to increase its market share from the 5% share it currently has. This ambitious growth plan will require significant investment in hiring more staff and potentially opening new gym locations across the country. The expansion is expected to bring substantial benefits to local communities, offering competitively priced fitness classes and gym instruction, thus promoting health and wellness on a larger scale. However, this growth plan poses several strategic decisions, particularly in how to scale up the business effectively and efficiently.

To achieve their national expansion goal, Stabler Gyms is weighing up two primary growth strategies: continuing organic growth or acquiring a competitor gym. Organic growth would involve opening new locations gradually, utilising their established brand reputation and operational expertise. On the other hand, acquiring a competitor could provide a faster route to a national presence, offering immediate access to new markets and customer bases. However, it also comes with financial and other risks. Richard has highlighted that there may be integration challenges and potential cultural clashes, particularly if the other gym does not have the same values as him. Richard and Vikram must carefully consider these options to ensure sustainable and successful growth for Stabler Gyms.

Topic 1

EXAMINATION PRACTICE

1. Which of the following is a financial reward for a business. [1]
   A – Personal satisfaction
   B – Profit
   C – Sense of achievement
   D – Wages

2. Which of the following is an advantage of becoming a public limited company? [1]
   A – Can raise large amounts of finance through selling shares to the public
   B – Financial accounts are available for public viewing
   C – Only invited individuals can become shareholders
   D – Owners have unlimited liability

3. Identify **two** purposes of business enterprise. [2]

4. Explain **one** drawback to a business of setting up as a partnership. [2]

5. Explain **one** reason why businesses have different objectives. [2]

6. Explain **one** way in which suppliers can impact a business. [2]

For the following questions, you must refer to the case study on the previous page.

7. Explain **one** entrepreneurial characteristic that Richard showed in setting up Stabler Gyms. [2]

8. Explain **one** risk that Richard and Vikram face in running Stabler Gyms. [2]

9. Analyse **one** benefit in setting up Stabler Gyms as a private limited company. [3]

10. Analyse **one** reason why Richard conducted thorough planning when setting up Stabler Gyms. [3]

11. Analyse **one** reward that the owners of Stabler Gym hope to achieve. [3]

12. Explain which stakeholder group will be most impacted by Stabler Gyms' growth. [2]

13. Evaluate whether Stabler Gyms should grow through horizontal integration. [9]

2.1

THE ROLE OF MARKETING

The marketing function in a business is all about selling the product. In order to do so the business needs to be able to know who their customers are and to understand them, whilst also ensuring that they inform the customers about the products they have available

The purpose of marketing within business

There are three purposes of marketing:

Identify and understand customers

Business need to know who they are selling to:
- How old is the target market?
- What can they afford?
- Are they male or female?

This will be looked at in section 2.3

Inform customers

Businesses need to ensure they let potential customers know that their products are available.

This will be covered in more detail in section 2.4

Increase sales

This could be through:
- Having a better quality product
- Having a cheaper price
- Selling products in more outlets
- Utilising promotions

Rebecca works as head of marketing at a technology company selling robotic lawnmowers.

Which **one** of the following is least likely to be part of her role? [1]

- A: Offering sales promotions to increase winter sales
- B: Researching a better design for the product
- C: Social media advertising to homeowners with gardens
- D: Surveys to establish the type of person who might be interested in a mower

2. B.[1] *This is because a design team would focus on product development.*

18 ClearRevise

2.2

MARKET RESEARCH

Satisfying customer needs is the key to success. The main reasons for carrying out **market research** are to find out information about who the customers are, where they are, what they want and when they want it.

Purpose of market research

A business must understand the needs of their customers to survive. Those that don't, have an increased risk of failure as customers will not buy from them. Other purposes include:

- To find out whether there is **demand** for a product.
- To identify **trends** in sales and consumer tastes.
- To help identify the demographic and geographic **target market**.
- To gain **feedback** from the customers so that a product can be altered to better meet their needs.
- To identify **gaps in the market** so that a business can produce a product that will have few competitors.
- To **understand competitors** so that the business is aware of alternative products and the strength of potential rivals.

> A product may be a physical good or a service.

Explain **two** benefits to a business of understanding changes in customer needs. [2]

Understanding changes will allow a business to adapt their products so the needs of customers are met.[1] This will help to maintain, or increase, sales.[1]

Another benefit is that they will then be able to build up customer loyalty.[1] This is because the business is providing goods/services that the customers actually want.[1]

OCR GCSE **Business**

19

2.2

PRIMARY MARKET RESEARCH METHODS

Primary market research is new information that is collected first-hand by a business. It includes asking people to fill out a **questionnaire**, undertaking an interview with a potential customer, **trialling** a product and holding **focus groups**.

Primary market research

Questionnaire: A relatively low-cost type of survey whereby a set of questions is distributed by mail, online or in person, for large samples of potential customers to fill in. Anonymous responses can help yield more honest answers and they can be completed independently so responses aren't swayed by group opinions. Quantitative data will usually be collected.

Interview: A further type of survey whereby an interviewer asks in depth questions either by phone or in person. This allows the business to gain detailed qualitative information, but there will be a limited sample.

Focus group: A small group of people who are selected to give their opinion on a particular product or aspect of the business. Feedback is immediate and follow up questions can be asked to gain detailed deeper qualitative information, but only a limited number of people will be involved. Focus groups are time-consuming to arrange and conduct, and participants will usually need to be paid a fee for their attendance.

Trialling: A business may sell a product for a limited period in a certain geographical area. This saves money as it is less expensive than a full release and allows them to see how it sells, indicating future demand. However, the usefulness of this method is dependent on whether the people trialling the product are representative of the target market.

Benefits

- The information collected will be up to date.
- The questions can be tailored to ask specific questions relevant to the business.
- It allows the business to have direct contact with existing and potential customers.

Drawbacks

- It can be time consuming to collect.
- The research is open to potential bias, depending on the sample used.
- Often more expensive.

George is an experienced gardener with many loyal customers. He is considering setting up a specialist lawn care service as a sole trader. Recommend whether George should use questionnaires or interviews to gauge customer needs and demand. [3]

Interviews would be relatively easy[1] if he included his current gardening customers and spoke to them as he saw them.[1] He could also gather more in-depth information into their needs and wants regarding lawn care.[1]

Questionnaires would be best[1] as he could hand them out to existing customers and through nearby letter boxes on his rounds.[1] This would collect data from a larger sample and allow people the time to consider their responses without pressure from George.[1]

2.2

SECONDARY MARKET RESEARCH METHODS

Secondary market research involves gathering data that already exists as it has been collected by someone else. Examples include reading newspapers and magazine, looking at census statistics, researching websites and using internal data.

Secondary market research

Benefits
- It is usually cheaper than primary research.
- It can be less time consuming because information is found more easily.

Drawbacks
- The information gathered may not be specific or relevant to the business.
- The information may be out of date.

Newspapers and magazines: A business can ascertain current trends and fashions from articles. They may also find information on new technologies, marketing ideas and competitor products.

Census statistics: Census data provides a business with data on UK households. This will provide a business with income statistics as well as occupations and information on the number of people living in each household.

Websites: A business can look at a competitor's website to see what they are selling and what prices they are charging.

Internal data: This is using data that the business has previously collected, such as past sales figures.

> Respond to questions such as this with a valid point, supported by a reason relating to the scenario for the application[APP] mark. The final mark comes from a further development mark for analysis[AN] relating to your initial point.

MFH Plastics manufacture plastic bottles for drinks companies. The managers are conducting some research so that they can determine what their level of demand might be in the coming years. Mark, the CEO of the firm, has decided that he will look at the accounts from the past three years in order to predict future sales.

Analyse **one** drawback to MFH Plastics of using internal data as a method of research. [3]

One drawback is that internal data can be outdated.[1] This is because Mark is using old accounts data from the past three years.[APP] There is no guarantee that past trends will continue in the future and sales levels may be different.[AN]

OCR GCSE **Business**

2.2

APPROPRIATENESS OF RESEARCH METHODS

When researching a market, a business will have to decide what combination of **primary and secondary research** methods will be most appropriate to their situation.

How appropriate different methods and sources of market research are for different business purposes

The decision as to which sources a business uses will be determined by the following factors:

Budgets:
Some, often smaller, businesses will have a relatively small amount to spend on market research, so may have to use as much secondary data as possible. Whereas others can afford to spend large amounts on primary research.

The information and data required:
If it's opinions on a product, then a focus group or interview might be best. If it's information about the makeup of the local population, then a business may just use secondary population data.

Factors affecting choice of research method

The proximity of customers:
If the target markets are not physically in the local area then a business may have to use an online questionnaire in order to get their opinions, rather than a focus group. Local magazines and papers may give some information on the general area.

When the information is needed:
Collecting primary research from potential customers and then analysing the results can take a long time. Information can be obtained a lot faster by utilising secondary market research methods.

2.2

USE AND INTERPRETATION OF DATA

Businesses will use the information and data that they collect to help inform decision making. The data collected can be categorised as either **qualitative** or **quantitative**.

Qualitative data

Qualitative data is based on people's feelings, judgements and opinions and cannot be expressed in numerical form. It is gained by asking open-ended questions, for example, 'Why do you like this product?'

Advantage
- Provides detailed information. This is because it allows the researcher to explore deeply into people's opinions through discussions and conversations.

Drawbacks
- Difficult to analyse in graphs and charts.
- The person analysing the data may show bias.

Quantitative data

Quantitative data is data that is collected in numerical form. It is usually captured through the use of closed questions, such as 'yes' / 'no' questions, those requiring a score on a scale or 1 to 10 for example, and multiple-choice questions.

Advantage
- Because it's in numerical form, it is a lot easier than qualitative data to analyse as it can be shown in charts and graphs.

Drawback
- Doesn't always allow a business to know exactly what a customer thinks, because it lacks specific opinions from customers.

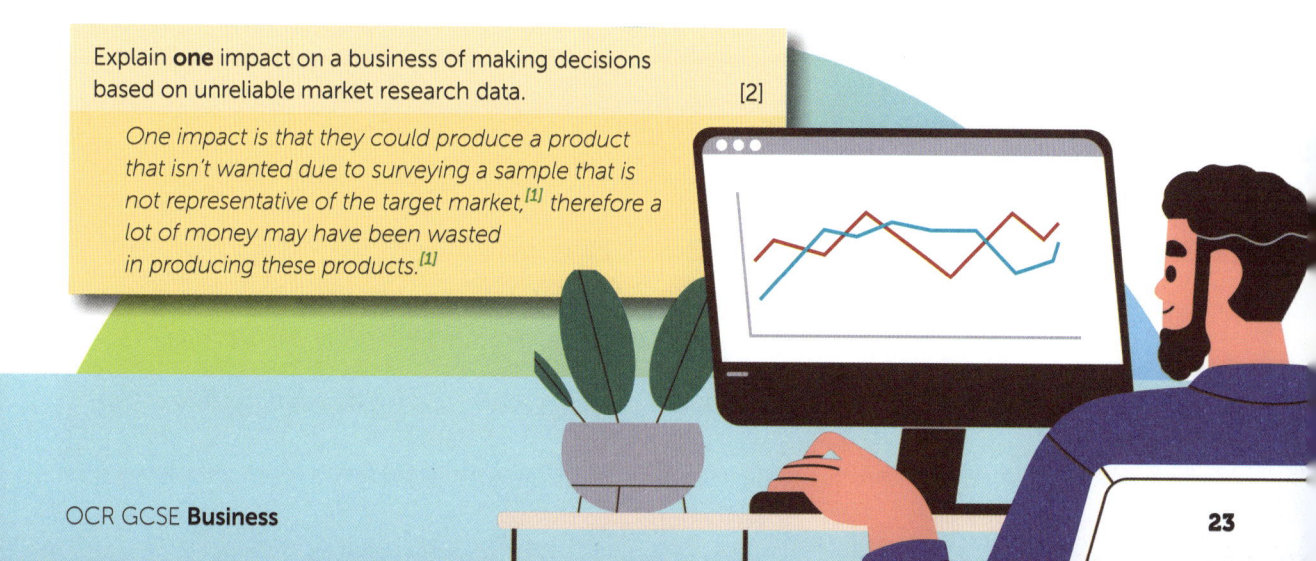

Explain **one** impact on a business of making decisions based on unreliable market research data. [2]

> One impact is that they could produce a product that isn't wanted due to surveying a sample that is not representative of the target market,[1] therefore a lot of money may have been wasted in producing these products.[1]

OCR GCSE **Business**

2.3

MARKET SEGMENTATION

Market segmentation involves grouping customers together based on shared characteristics, wants and needs. Once a target segment is identified, the business must decide what their needs are and where to place a new product in the market.

How a business segments the market

Location
Grouping customers together based on where they live enables a business to focus on selling to people in certain areas.

Lifestyle
Grouping customers based on their hobbies and interests or based on the way they live their lives (e.g. health conscious and active) can help identify more relevant customers.

Age
Grouping customers based on how old they are.

Gender
A business may decide to segment the market based on gender, as it is common that they have different needs.

Income
People can be grouped on income bracket (how much money they earn). A product may be more suitable for a budget or luxury market.

Why businesses segment the market

To differentiate from competitors: Offering a product that meets the specific needs of a group of customers will help a business stand out from its rivals.

To develop products that fit a specific groups' needs: This allows a business to charge more for their product, as customers will be willing to pay more for a product that is unique in some way.

To promote a product more effectively: A business can promote in places where their target market will notice them. For instance, a company selling golf clubs can place an advert in a golf magazine or base their store near several courses.

Explain **one** drawback to a business from segmenting the market. [2]

The market will become narrower.[1] *This means that the business will restrict the number of potential customers that it is aiming at.*[1]
It can be more expensive to segment the market.[1] *This is because they will have to adapt their product to meet the individual needs of the segment they are aiming at.*[1]

THE MARKETING MIX: PRODUCT

The marketing mix is a combination of four factors – 'the four Ps' (product, price, place and promotion) which a business uses in order to persuade customers to buy their product. The mix will change over time and each element has an influence on the others. When a business has found out the needs of its target market, it must design, invent or innovate a product to meet those needs.

Design, invention and innovation

Design – The design of the product incorporates the functionality, its features, and its appearance. If what is produced is unique then it will be differentiated from competitor products.

Invention – When a business comes up with a product that is new to the market.

Innovation – When a business improves an existing product with new functionality, features or materials.

1. Explain the importance of designing a product that meets the needs of the target market. [2]

   It is important that the design meets their needs so that they are satisfied with the product.[1] This will mean that they will be more likely to recommend it / return and purchase it again.[1]

Product range

A business may choose to have a wide product range for the following reasons:
- To spread risk: By diversifying with more products in more than one market, a business is less at risk of failure should sales in one product or market start to decline.
- To increase sales: By having more products available to purchase, a business hopes that its sales will improve.

2. Explain **one** drawback to a business of manufacturing and producing a wide product range. [2]

   If one product develops a bad reputation, it can damage the reputation of the other products.[1] This may lead to lower sales across all the range.[1]

   Other answers could include: increased workload; more difficult to control and coordinate; the business' focus is diluted; they may experience diseconomies of scale.

2.4

PRODUCT LIFE CYCLE

Every product has a life span. To ensure a business continues to be successful it needs to understand the life cycle of its products. If it believes that the sales of a product may soon start to fall, the business can take some actions to extend its life span.

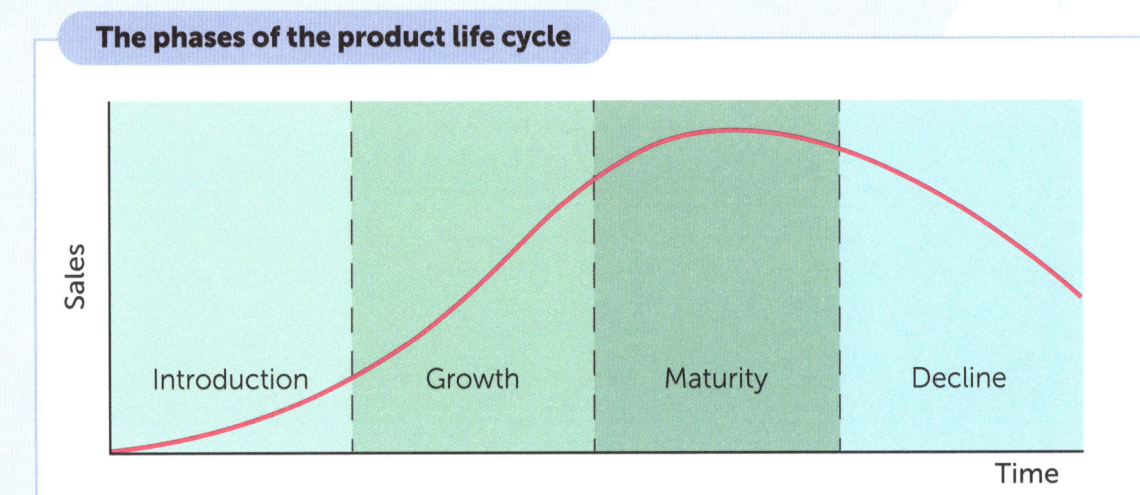

The phases of the product life cycle

Sales vs Time graph showing curve rising through Introduction, Growth, peaking at Maturity, and falling in Decline.

Introduction	Growth	Maturity	Decline
The product is launched onto the market. Sales start to increase. Cash-flow is likely to remain negative as the business must heavily promote the product to develop awareness of it.	Sales will start to rise more rapidly after a successful launch as customers become more familiar with the product. As sales start to rise, cash-flow starts to become positive.	Sales levels and cash-flow are at their highest. However, growth in sales will start to slow down. The market may become saturated as more competitors enter the market.	Sales of the product decrease. This may be because the product is outdated. If this continues, the business may decide to withdraw the product.

2.4

THE MARKETING MIX: PRICE

The price a business charges plays an important role in developing a successful marketing mix. A business must choose which pricing strategy to adopt, but there are many factors that will influence this decision.

Pricing methods

Skimming

A business will set a high price for its product as it is launched into the market. This may be because it is a technologically superior product, of higher quality than the rest of the market, or it is highly differentiated in some way, meaning people are prepared to pay more for it. The price will fall as competing products emerge.

Penetration pricing

A business will sell a product at a low price. This may be how they are differentiating their product. It is likely that this strategy will be used in the mass market with the aim to sell higher volumes to a greater proportion of the total market.

Competitor pricing

A business will set a price for its products based on the price that rival businesses charge. They will commonly match the price of their rivals, or just undercut them.

Promotional pricing

This is where a business will reduce prices in order to receive a boost in sales. It is often used by businesses to sell off old stock.

Cost-plus pricing

The cost of producing a product is calculated and then a percentage margin is added to establish a selling price. This is to ensure that the business makes a profit on each sale.

BlueWave Express have unveiled a new transport link between the seaside towns of AquaBay and OceanShores. They plan to run a direct service between the two major tourist areas. Their rivals provide a similar service that takes longer as they make many stops on the way. A news article said "BlueWave will now transport tourists seamlessly from one breathtaking town to another in half the time of anyone else."

Analyse **one** benefit to BlueWave of using price skimming for its new route. [3]

> Tourists will be happy to pay a higher price for a quicker route between AquaBay and OceanShores[1] because it will save them time as the new route only takes half the time of others.[APP] As a result BlueWave will experience increased revenues.[AN]

OCR GCSE **Business**

2.4 THE MARKETING MIX: PROMOTION

Promotion helps to create awareness of a business and its products. Its purpose is to instil the desire in a customer to want to purchase a product. A business can do this through **point of sale** promotion or through **advertising**.

Point of sale promotion

Price reductions

This includes discounts and special offers such as buy one get one free.

Benefit: Customers feel that they are getting a bargain.

Drawback: Profit margins will be reduced.

Competitions

When a person buys a certain product, they are entered into a prize draw or other competition. Typical prizes could be other gift vouchers, products, holidays or experiences.

Benefit: Customers buy more of the product in order to enter / increase their chances in the competition.

Drawback: Prizes can be expensive to purchase and may offset any increase in revenue.

Loss leaders

The price of a product is so low that the business actually makes a loss on the sale of each product.

Benefit: Customers buy other products when they visit the store to buy the loss leader.

Drawback: Business makes a loss on the sale of each product sold.

Free samples

Samples of product are given free of charge to potential customers to try. This is often used in the cosmetics and food and drink industries.

Benefit: It allows customers to sample the product and therefore they may feel inclined to buy it.

Drawback: Could give away a lot of the product and still not make many sales.

Advertising

Communication is used to inform potential customers about products and to persuade them to buy. It can take many forms and not all methods will be suitable for every business.

Social media

Benefits
- Growing numbers of people use social media.
- The business can have a global reach.
- Low-cost method.
- Can target specific types of individual.
- Quick to update.

Drawbacks
- Adverts may get ignored as customers scroll past them.
- Businesses may find it difficult to get their advert to stand out as there are lots of competing businesses doing the same.

Websites

Benefits
- Cost effective and can be easily updated.
- Reach customers who already have an interest in the business.
- Video and audio can be included to show the products.
- Adverts can be easily found using search engines.
- Business can obtain the analytics of customer visits to the site.

Drawbacks
- Customers may have to know about the business in order to visit the site (unless the business is well positioned in search engines).
- Have to pay someone to keep the website up to date.

Print media

Benefits
- Can target specific publications read by the target market.
- Can show images to showcase the product.

Drawbacks
- Can be expensive to advertise in publications that have a large reader base.

Television

Benefits
- Potential to reach a very large audience.
- Can have a high impact visually and showcase the product.
- Can target specific groups.

Drawbacks
- Often a very expensive form of advertising.
- Customers could ignore the advert, or switch channels.

Radio

Benefits
- Can reach a wide target market.
- Radio stations can be selected to reach certain geographical areas or certain audiences.
- Can select time of advert to suit certain audiences.
- Can reach customers doing other activities.

Drawbacks
- Listeners cannot see the products being advertised.
- Customers cannot refer back to the adverts.

OCR GCSE **Business**

2.4

THE MARKETING MIX: PLACE

Place considers a business' location and the method of distribution used. This determines how the product gets to the end consumer.

Methods of distribution

A **distribution channel** is the route that a product takes from where it is manufactured to where it is sold to the end consumer. **Physical distribution** is distributing a physical good. This could be direct or could involve the use of a retailer or wholesaler.

Direct

Direct distribution is employed by businesses that sell their product directly to the customer. This allows the producer to engage in direct communication with the customer so they will know if there is a problem. This creates a better understanding of the changing needs of the customers so products can be adapted if needed. Many **e-commerce** businesses will sell directly to customers via their own website.

Retailers

Some manufacturers will sell their products to a **retailer**. This is a 'middle-man' who buys products from the producer in larger quantities and then sells them on for a higher price to the end consumer. The retailer is a more convenient place for a customer to buy from.

Wholesalers

A wholesaler is a large distribution company that will purchase products in bulk at a discounted rate from many different manufacturers and then sell them on to smaller retailers. This is a more efficient way for a manufacturing firm to distribute its products as it makes one large delivery instead of lots of smaller deliveries to all the retailers that stock its products.

---

1. Explain **one** advantage to a producer of choosing to include a wholesaler in its distribution channel. [2]

   One advantage is that the producer's transport costs will be lower.[1] This is because the wholesaler will buy in bulk from the producer so goods can be delivered all at once.[1]

Digital distribution

Technological developments have meant that some products can now be delivered digitally. **Digital distribution** is used where goods and services are accessed or downloaded by a customer from a website or application. Common products that are delivered in this way include:
- Media – books, newspapers and magazines.
- Entertainment – films, music and TV programmes.
- Financial services – insurance and banking.

Digital distribution should not be confused with e-commerce as online sales still involves physical distribution.

2. Explain **two** benefits to a business of delivering its products digitally. [4]

One advantage is that consumers can buy and receive the product 24/7.[1] *This may mean that the business will receive increased sales.*[1]

Another advantage is that a business may benefit from reduced costs.[1] *This is because they do not have the costs of a physical shop or have to pay transportation costs.*[1]

Drawbacks of digital distribution

- Some products cannot be distributed digitally.
- Some customers who do not own the necessary technology to make the purchase will not be able to buy the product.
- There is a risk that downloaded content can be shared by customers illegally, therefore reducing the number of sales that a business may make.

OCR GCSE **Business**

2.4

THE MARKETING MIX

For a business to be successful, its needs to develop an integrated **marketing mix** as this will have an influence on a business' competitive advantage. Each of the elements is inter-related and must complement each other.

How the four Ps of the marketing mix work together

All the elements of the marketing mix will influence each other. If a business decides to produce a new, high-quality, luxury and innovative product utilising the latest technology, the product will influence the other factors in the following ways:

Price: The product is likely to cost a lot to manufacture and the price will need to be set high to reflect this and provide a satisfactory margin.

Promotion: The promotion strategies used must be appropriate given the product is of a high quality and likely to be targeted at the premium market.

Place: To uphold the product's superior image, it must be sold in suitable establishments that enhance this image. Distribution is not likely to be extensive in order to protect the luxury image.

Explain **one** way that promotion may impact on the price element of the marketing mix. [2]

A business may decide to conduct a free promotion using regular posts on social media rather than using TV advertising.[1] This will mean that the overall business costs are lower so the business can charge a lower price for its product.[1]

Alternative answer:

A promotional campaign may be trying to portray an image of luxury and the price of the product needs to reflect this.[1] Consequently, the business may use a price skimming strategy.[1]

How the four Ps of the marketing mix work together

The marketing mix is used to help a business make key decisions about the products that it sells.

1. Price

This element of the marketing mix helps a business to make decisions about the most appropriate pricing strategy to use, A business must set a price that enables it to make a profit. Therefore, it is important that an entrepreneur is aware of all the costs involved. A new start-up will often sell their products at a low price in order to attract people to purchase their products. A product that is of a superior quality may be able to be priced highly compared to competitor products. Businesses will look at what prices consumers are willing to pay, what their competitors charge and what the current market conditions are like.

2. Product

After conducting market research, a business will know the needs of their customers. The product element helps a business to meet those needs through its features, design and function. Through analysing their product portfolio and utilising analysis tools such as the product life cycle, businesses can make decisions about whether to introduce new products, update existing products or stop producing unprofitable ones. The product element also helps a business to consider what will make its products different from others on the market.

3. Promotion

A business needs to promote itself to raise customer awareness of the products that are available. This element will help make decisions about appropriate promotional strategies to use. In doing so, businesses will consider their budget, who their target audience is and what it is that they want to achieve. This will help the business to implement a relevant promotional strategy. This helps to increase sales and build a brand image. There are many forms of promotion which include advertising, special offers and public relations.

4. Place

A business must think about distribution; the place element allows a business to make decisions about how they will get the product to the customer. Within this element, businesses have to decide whether to sell directly to the customer, either by having a physical location or via the Internet, or they could choose to use wholesalers and retailers. It will help them to make decisions surrounding the location of the business and logistics, to ensure that the product gets to the customer in a timely fashion.

OCR GCSE **Business**

2.4
INTERPRETATION OF MARKET DATA

Businesses will use the information and data that they collect to help inform decision making. This provides details on changes in demand, the business' market share and the target market. It also informs changes in the product and evaluates the effects of promotional strategies.

Changes in demand

Market data can show whether demand for a particular product is increasing or falling. This will help a business in the following ways:
- It will help make pricing decisions. Does the business need to drop the price because sales have started to fall?
- It will help make decisions on promotional strategies, for example, do they need to advertise more, should more social media be used?
- If the data suggests that demand is declining and it is irreversible, should the business introduce a new product?

Changes in target market

A product may not be selling enough to a current target market or resonating well enough with those who have made a purchase. People may also find new ways of using a product that the business had not previously thought of. In these instances, the business may choose to change the target market. This will have knock-on effects on the marketing mix.

Market share

Market share is defined as the percentage of the total sales made in a market by one business. It can be calculated using the formula:

$$\text{Market share} = (\text{Sales of the product} \div \text{Total market sales}) \times 100$$

Market data will help a business to calculate what their market share is and how this has changed over the past few years. This will help trigger strategies to further increase their market share or find ways to reverse a declining market share.

Accidental inventions: Play-Doh started out (in white only) as a wallpaper cleaner in the 1930s.

It wasn't until the 1950s that the product started to be used in schools as modelling clay. Different colours were then produced and the target market shifted from adult homeowners to children, parents and schools.

Product changes

Market data will help a business to ascertain whether the customer needs have changed and what demand there is for new features. Improvements to competitor products may also influence change. This will help a business to decide:

- Whether to introduce a new product to the market.
- Whether to adapt an existing product to continue to meet the needs of the customers.

Effect of promotion

Looking at sales data will help a business to assess whether its promotion has been effective or not. They can assess whether it has been money well spent given any change in sales or whether they need to make changes to their promotion strategy.

Asra is the owner of the Market Cafe in North East England. She has always prided herself on offering homemade delicacies baked using the finest ingredients. Recently, her keen eye for market trends revealed a growing vegan population in the local area. Acting on this insight, Asra launched a vibrant social media campaign highlighting the cafe's commitment to quality and freshness, and its diverse, vegan-friendly menu. The response was positive and her posts were shared widely, leading to a noticeable increase in sales.

Analyse **one** benefit to the Market Café of using market data to create new products. [3]

Asra may use market data to identify trends[1] in the market, such as the increase in the vegan population in the local area.[APP] This will hep Asra to introduce more vegan products to the market, possibly increasing sales.[AN]

OCR GCSE **Business**

CASE STUDY

Porkey's Ltd., a family-run business nestled in the heart of Norfolk, has carved out a niche in the cured meats market. Specialising in free-range chorizo, salami, air-dried beef and pork, and flavoured jerky, the company's journey began with meticulous primary market research. The founders attended local farmers' markets, interviewing attendees to gauge their interest and opinions on premium cured meats. This hands-on approach revealed a promising gap in the market, suggesting a strong local demand for their high-quality meats. Additionally, census data showed that the local population had a higher-than-average income, reinforcing the potential for success.

Porkey's strategy involves selling their products through various channels. They supply large regional retailers, including nationwide supermarket chains, while also maintaining a direct-to-consumer approach at farmers' markets and trade fairs. One particularly successful promotional tactic has been offering free samples at these markets, with data showing that 73% of people who taste the meats make a purchase. This strategy not only boosts sales but also allows customers to experience the exceptional quality and flavour that Porkey's is renowned for. The company takes immense pride in using only free-range pork and rare breed British beef, ensuring the highest welfare standards for their livestock.

Looking to expand their offerings, Porkey's is considering introducing a line of charcuterie boards available for online purchase. Market data indicates a growing trend of people opting to host dinner parties at home rather than dining out, suggesting a strong demand for such products. Sales analysis has shown a remarkable 42% increase over the past two years, reinforcing their confidence in this new venture. The charcuterie boards will feature their finest cured meats and other high-quality local ingredients, justifying a premium pricing strategy. To promote this new range, they are contemplating advertising on local radio or using their own website, aiming to capture the attention of customers looking for the best in local produce.

Topic 2

EXAMINATION PRACTICE

1. A retailer has increased their spending on promotion, which has led to an increase in sales from £250,000 to £300,000. What is the percentage increase in sales? [1]
   A – 16.67%
   B – 20%
   C – 50%
   D – 83.33%

2. An entrepreneur is thinking of setting up a Barbershop in their local area. What is an example of qualitative data they could use? [1]
   A – The number of adults who live and work in the local area.
   B – The number of people who walk past their proposed location a day.
   C – The opinions of the local population on hair styles.
   D – The prices charged by local rival barbershops.

3. Identify **two** stages of the product life cycle. [2]

4. Explain **one** reason why a business may have a wide product range. [2]

5. Explain **one** benefit to a business from using a penetration pricing strategy. [2]

6. Explain **one** way in which the product element of the marketing mix, impacts the price. [2]

For the following questions, you must refer to the case study on the previous page.

7. Explain **one** reason why Porkey's used interviews as part of their research. [2]

8. Explain **one** way that Porkey's can segment the market. [2]

9. Analyse **one** reason why Porkey's uses retailers to distribute its products. [3]

10. Analyse **one** reason why Porkey's gives out free samples. [3]

11. Analyse **one** benefit to Porkey's of using secondary research. [3]

12. Recommend whether advertising on the radio or their own website would be the most appropriate method for Porkey's to promote their charcuterie boards. [3]

13. Evaluate whether Porkey's should introduce the new line of charcuterie boards. [9]

OCR GCSE **Business**

3.1

THE ROLE OF HUMAN RESOURCES

The role of Human Resources (HR) is pivotal in managing a company's most valuable asset: its people. HR is responsible for all aspects of managing the staff, from **recruitment** to **motivation** and **training**.

The purpose of human resources in business

In business it is the purpose of the HR function to:
- Determine the workforce needs.
- Communicate with employees. (**Page 42**.)
- Recruit and select the most appropriate employees. (**Page 44**.)
- Motivate and retain employees. (**Page 46**.)
- Induct and train employees. (**Page 48**.)

Determining the workforce needs

The HR function must determine the needs of the business so that they can create a workforce plan. This will include determining:
- The number of workers needed.
- The type of workers needed, in terms of skills required.
- When the workers will be needed – are they required full time, or just to cover a short period of time?
- How the business will get the best out of their workers.

Explain **one** reason why HR need to determine the workforce needs of a business. [2]

One reason is so that they can ensure they have the right number of staff.[1] This is because the business may have peak times where it needs more staff to help serve customers and determining this beforehand will ensure they have enough cover.[1]

38 ClearRevise

3.2

ORGANISATIONAL STRUCTURE

An **organisational structure** refers to the way in which a business is organised in terms of its employees. The structure selected by a business will have an impact on many issues such as employee motivation and communication.

Reasons for having an organisational structure

As a business grows, it becomes increasingly important to have a defined internal structure for the following reasons:

It helps to improve the flow of communication: Having an internal structure makes the chain of command more obvious. Therefore, channels of communications are clearly defined.

Allows a business to function: An organisational structure will separate employees into functional areas, ensuring that all necessary aspects of business are covered.

Allows a business to organise its employees: Employees will understand their roles better in relation to other colleagues.

It shows how employees fit into the business: Employees can immediately see who their line manager is and which others they are responsible for.

It helps in monitoring employees: All managers will know who they are responsible for, therefore they can ensure they support and guide their team.

Ways of working

Many businesses are changing the way they ask employees to work. Flexible working arrangements are much more common, and this can suit both the individual and the business.

Full-time: Usually classed as someone who works 35 hours a week or more (an individual cannot work more than 48 hours per week due to regulations in place).

Part-time: Employees that work fewer than 35 hours per week are classed as part-time, but they have exactly the same rights as a full-time member of staff.

Flexible hours: An employee will have to work a certain number of hours a week, but there is flexibility as to when those hours can be completed.

Temporary: A business may employ people for a defined period of time to cover busy periods or staff absence.

Working from home: When an employee completes work whilst at home, there are savings on business costs by not having to provide office space.

Working while mobile: People can work whilst they are on the move, such as those that work whilst travelling or on holiday.

Self-employed: Freelancers are self-employed people who are hired by a business to work on a specific project for a period of time. They are usually highly qualified experts in their field. Businesses do not need to provide training, pensions, sick pay or holiday pay, and can use freelancers as and when they are required. This can lower costs.

OCR GCSE **Business**

3.2

ORGANISATIONAL STRUCTURE

Organisational structure

```
                        Director
            ┌──────────────┼──────────────┬──────────────┐
       Marketing       Finance          HR          Operations
        Manager        Manager        Manager        Manager
    ┌──────┼──────┐
  Sales  Promotions  Overseas Sales
Supervisor  Manager   Supervisor
    │        │            │
3 assistants 6 assistants 5 assistants
```

Delayering involves reducing the number of levels within the hierarchy by removing elements from the organisational structure. This could reduce costs or improve the speed and quality of communication, as the chain of command would be shorter.

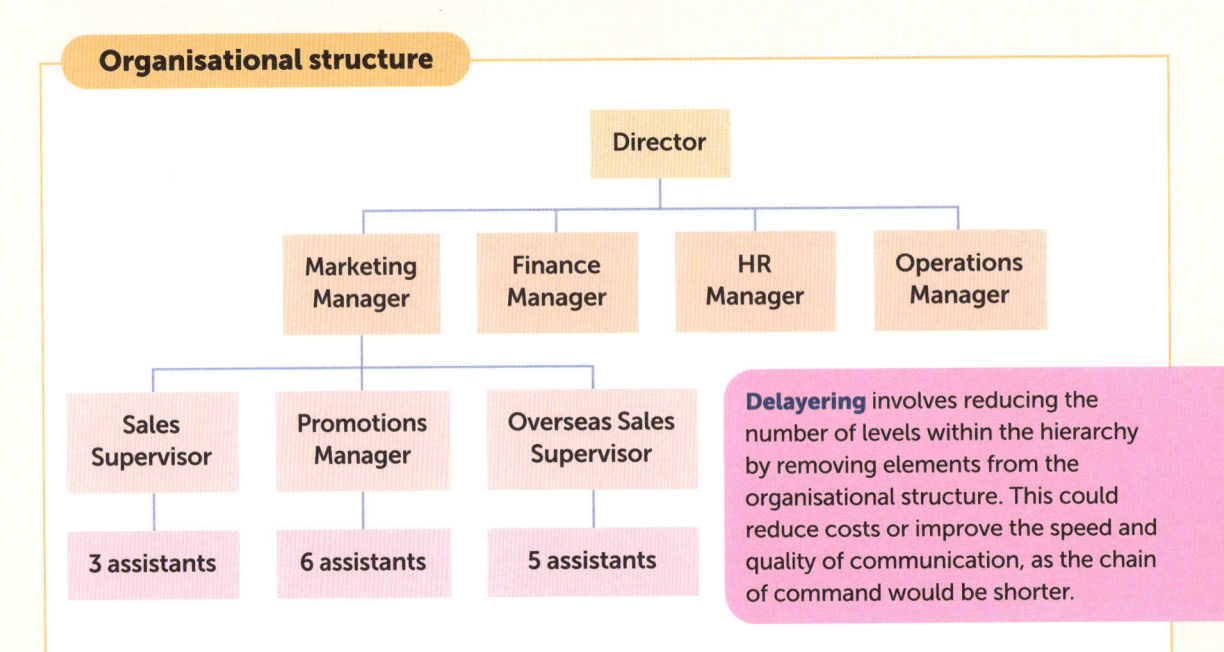

Span of control

The **span of control** is the number of people that a line manager is directly responsible for. A wide span of control means a manager has many subordinates to manage. In the example above, the Marketing Manager has a span of control of 3 that they are directly responsible for.

Chain of command

The **chain of command** is the line of authority within a business along which communication passes. For instance, in the example above, if the Director wanted to pass on details of new marketing objectives for the business, they will pass instructions to the Marketing Manager. In turn, they would then pass these on to the Supervisors, who would then inform the assistants they are responsible for. Effective communication becomes more difficult as the chain gets longer.

Delegation

Delegation means to pass authority and responsibility to colleagues lower down in the hierarchy. For instance, in the example above, the Director may delegate all decisions regarding marketing, to the Marketing Manager.

Subordinate

Workers that a line manager is responsible for. In the example above the Sales Supervisor is the **subordinate** of the Marketing Manager.

Authority

The power to make decisions and give instructions to those employees they are in charge of. In the chart above the Director has the most **authority**.

Tall vs flat structure

Tall structure

- Many levels of hierarchy, therefore a longer chain of command.
- Promotional opportunities for staff.
- Managers have a narrow span of control.
- Slower communication flow.

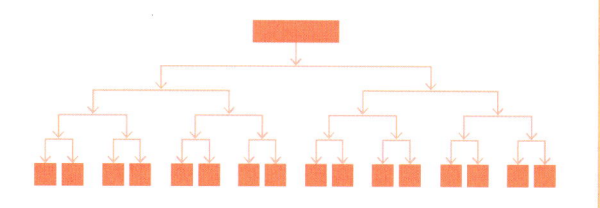

Flat structure

- Fewer levels of hierarchy, so there will be a shorter chain of command.
- Managers have wide spans of control.
- More delegation and authority given to staff.
- Communication is quicker as there are fewer levels in the hierarchy.

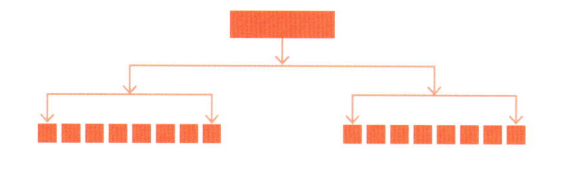

Why businesses have different organisational structures

There are several reasons why businesses have different organisational structures:

1. The size of the business – larger businesses tend to have more layers.

2. The nature of the business – creative industries tend to have flatter structures.

3. The business objectives.

4. The style of management – some managers prefer a hands-off approach and will allow more freedom to employees.

5. Skills and expertise of employees – a flat structure is more suitable when employees are highly skilled and self-motivated.

6. Different ways of working – a business may decide that all employees working in one function (e.g. Marketing) should be organised together, so these tend to be taller structures.

Explain **one** reason why communication can impact a business' organisational structure. [2]

If it is important to have quick communication through the business, then a flat structure will be more appropriate.[1] This is because there is a shorter chain of command and fewer layers for messages to pass through.[1]

COMMUNICATION IN BUSINESS

If there is effective **communication** in a business, then everyone should be aware of what it is that the business is trying to achieve. They will also know exactly what their role is and what is required of them. A lot of businesses will now rely on digital communication.

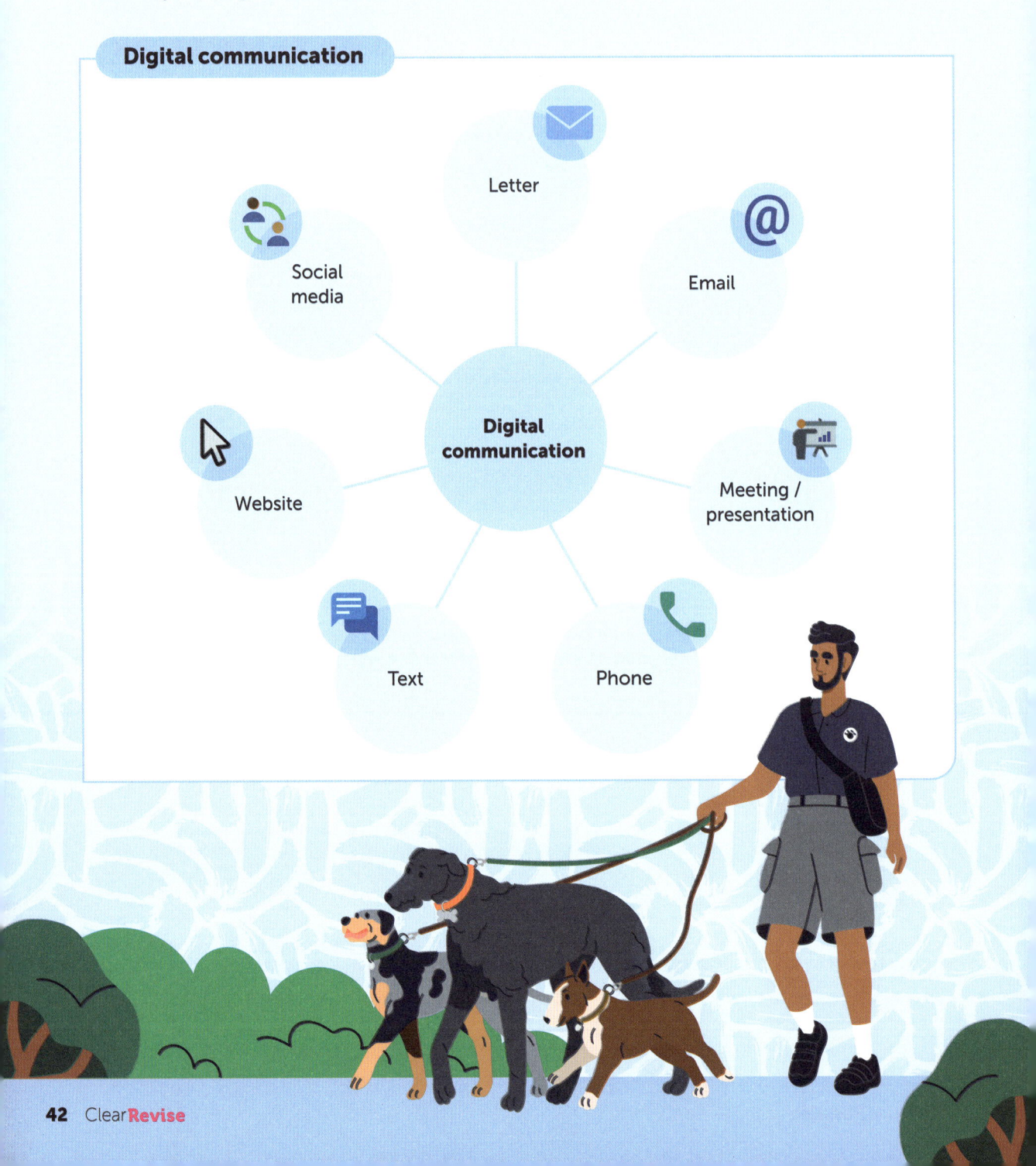

Digital communication

- Letter
- Email
- Meeting / presentation
- Phone
- Text
- Website
- Social media

Digital communication

42 ClearRevise

The importance of business communications

Effective communication between a business and its stakeholders is vital, as it ensures that messages are clear, and passed on through the right channels, helping to avoid any confusion. This benefits a business in the following ways:

- It helps a manager and employees to minimise mistakes and misunderstandings.
- Confidential information has less chance of being misplaced, misused or leaked.
- It will help to ensure that all employees understand what their role is and what the business expects of them.
- It ensures that everyone is clear as to what the business' aims and objectives are.
- If employees communicate well with customers, it will ensure that they have sufficient information about the product they are buying.

Inefficient or excessive communication can have an impact on the motivation of the workforce and efficiency in the following ways:

- Too little communication means that an employee may not understand their role and be demotivated as a result, whilst other jobs may not be completed properly.
- Too much communication may cause employees to feel overwhelmed and stressed, whilst also leading to important information being missed or overlooked.

Digital communication

Digital communication involves contacting colleagues or stakeholders, such as customers, electronically. This has changed the way that businesses communicate. Communication is now much quicker and can be very cost effective.

Digital communication is great until the technology it relies upon fails.

- Email and apps have enabled businesses to send and receive messages instantly at very little cost.
- Online meeting software has enabled people to meet and have face to face communication without the need to travel.
- Mobiles, laptops and tablets have enabled people to work and communicate with others when they are away from their usual place of work.

Harry runs a dog walking business in his local village. He has a number of regular clients who use him to look after their pets when they are away at work. He is popular with his clients as he is flexible in his approach and will work around the timings that suit the customer. He communicates with his customers digitally.

Explain **one** method Harry may use technology to communicate with his customers. [2]

> Harry may communicate with his customers via text.[1] He could use a messaging app to confirm the times that he is looking after their dogs.[APP]

OCR GCSE **Business**

3.4

RECRUITMENT AND SELECTION

When recruiting, a business must decide what role it needs to fill and what method they will use to recruit those required.

The need for recruitment

A business may need to recruit a new employee for one of the following reasons:
- When a business first becomes established.
- The business is growing.
- Replacing an employee that has left. This could be because they have accepted another job elsewhere, they have moved into retirement, or they have been dismissed.
- The current workforce does not possess the skills that the business needs.
- To cover a position on a temporary basis. An employee could be on maternity/paternity leave or could be on long term sickness absence.

Internal and external recruitment

Internal recruitment means a vacancy is filled with someone who already works in the business. **External recruitment** occurs when a business employs someone that does not already work for the organisation. The relative merits of each are below:

Internal

- ⊕ The employee will already know the business and the business them, so less induction training is needed.
- ⊕ Faster, easier, and cheaper way to recruit.
- ⊕ Promoting from within can be motivating for employees
- ⊖ Workers may lack the exact skills that the business needs.
- ⊖ Choice of who to appoint is restricted.

External

- ⊕ New employees may bring fresh ideas.
- ⊕ There may be a bigger pool of potential applicants to choose from.
- ⊕ May be necessary if the vacancy has arisen due to growth of the business.
- ⊖ The business will know less about the person they select.
- ⊖ The person may not be able to start immediately.

---

1. Explain **one** drawback of externally recruiting an employee. [2]
2. Explain **one** drawback of internal recruitment to a business. [2]

1. The business will know less about the person they select than if they had recruited internally.[1] Therefore, they have a greater chance of making a mistake with the selection.[1]

2. The pool of internal employees may not have the exact skills that the business needs.[1] Therefore, they may have to pay more to train the employee that is selected for the role.[1]

The need for recruitment

As part of the recruitment process, a business will produce a job description and person specification.

- A **job description** is a document telling potential applicants all the details of the job itself including details such as the role, key duties, hours and salary.
- A **person specification** is a document that tells applicants about the skills and characteristics that are required to be able to complete the job.
- When someone applies for a job, they may also have to send in a **curriculum vitae** (**CV**). This is a document that details the education, qualifications and employment history of the applicant.

Methods of selection

Once a business has decided who it will recruit, what the job is and the type of person they want, they have to select the best candidate. To do this they will utilise the following methods:

Application form	An application form is created by the business and completed by the applicants. A business can decide what information it wants to gather in order to compare applicants.
CV	A curriculum vitae is written by the applicant and sent to the business. It details the applicant's qualifications, skills and experiences.
Letter of application	This is written by the applicant to detail why they think they will be suitable for the job they've applied for.
Interviews	Some applicants are invited to an interview where they will be asked questions by the interviewer. It is used to assess a candidate's suitability for the job and to judge their character and communication skills.
Testing	Applicants may be asked to undertake some form of testing. This could be a skill specific to the role they have applied for, or a personality based test.
Group activities	Candidates may be asked to take part in some sort of group activity to assess how well they work with other people. It can also showcase a candidate's leadership capabilities.
References	A business will ask former employers, or people who have worked with the candidate previously, about their capabilities.

OCR GCSE **Business**

3.5

MOTIVATION AND RETENTION

Motivation can be defined as the reason an employee acts or behaves in a certain way. It is their desire or willingness to complete a task. To be successful, a business needs motivated staff who can be enthused or encouraged using financial or non-financial methods. Having motivated employees helps to improve staff **retention** rates.

Financial methods of motivation

Pay

This can either be through a salary (a fixed amount paid per year, usually split into monthly payments) or by a wage (an amount usually paid weekly to an employee in return for a set number of hours of work). Paying an employee a high salary can be motivating, but employees are also motivated by the prospect of incremental increases in salary over time. Employees paid by wage may be motivated to work overtime as they will then often receive an enhanced hourly rate for their efforts.

Bonus

A sum of money paid to an employee for achieving a target. It can also be paid to staff as a result of the business performing well. This motivates employees to help a business succeed as they are more likely to gain financially themselves.

Profit share

Using this method, employees are financially rewarded as they will receive a share of the business' profit alongside their usual salary or wage. They will be motivated to help the business perform better, as the more profit the business makes, the more they receive.

Fringe benefits

Fringe benefits: Perks that carry a financial value that are given to employees.

- Private health care
- Pension schemes
- Gym membership
- Company car
- Staff discount
- Free meals

1. Explain **one** way in which fringe benefits motivate employees. [2]

   Fringe benefits are motivational because they are additional perks given to employees on top of their wage / salary.[1] An example is offering an employee discount when buying the business' own products so they feel happier that they bought them for less money.[1]

46 ClearRevise

Non-financial methods of motivation

Praise

Employees can feel valued if their efforts are recognised by their line manager and the business' senior management.

Award schemes

Many businesses provide rewards for good work. This could be anything from vouchers, holidays, or a certificate. Some businesses offer 'Employee of the month' award schemes.

2. Explain how a positive working environment can motivate employees. [2]

Employees will feel part of a team,[1] therefore they enjoy coming to work and will be happier in their role.[1]

The importance of employee motivation

Motivation is important for a number of reasons:

- It helps to keep staff turnover low. Staff turnover is the percentage of the workforce who leave over a period of time.
- It can help to lower staff absence rates as employees enjoy coming to work.
- It helps to attract new employees. People will want to come and work for a business that looks after them.
- It can lead to employees providing better customer service, enhancing the business' reputation.
- It can lead to a more committed workforce who want to be involved in helping the business succeed, and as a result they may be more likely to provide new ideas.
- It can help to improve communication within the business.
- It can lead to an increase in the business' productivity.

The importance of employee retention

Employee retention is the goal of businesses to keep a hold of their workers rather than having them leave to work somewhere else. It is important that retention rates are high for a business.

3. Explain **two** reasons why employee retention is important for a business. [4]

Having high retention rates will mean that a business' recruitment costs will be low.[1] This means that the business can spend the money more effectively elsewhere, such as motivational packages.[1]

Retaining employees means that they will become more familiar with the business' customers,[1] meaning that they can continue to build relationships which will improve customer loyalty and company reputation.[1]

Saves time for HR and managers[1] as they do not have to spend time recruiting.[1]

It will reduce training costs[1] as the business will not have to spend time inducting new employees.[1]

High retention rates maintains an experienced workforce[1] which help a business to operate more efficiently.[1]

OCR GCSE **Business**

TRAINING AND DEVELOPMENT

Training can take many forms, but it is essential that all businesses conduct ongoing training so that employees can keep up to date with the latest developments.

Why businesses train their workers

Improve productivity: Training workers will enhance their skills and knowledge to help make them better at their jobs. This will increase efficiency and productivity where more work is completed in the same amount of time.

Staff retention: Employees who feel valued by a business are less likely to leave. Employees may also appreciate the training and development they are getting in their career, further increasing their loyalty and commitment to the business.

Good customer service: Well-informed employees are much more likely to deal with customers in an effective way, making sure that the customer's needs are fully met.

Skill shortages: A business can identify where their workers lack certain necessary skills, and train them in this area.

Motivation: By investing in training a member of staff, a business is giving that employee the opportunity to learn new skills and develop themselves. Learning can be extremely motivating for an employee, and they may feel more valued by the business.

Development of the business: Well-trained employees feel confident and valued. They will likely take greater care over the work they do and contribute suggestions for the benefit of the business. This will improve workflow and enhance the business' reputation, helping the business to grow.

Different training methods

Induction training

Induction training takes place when someone is new to the job. It allows them to become familiar with the business and its processes and objectives, as well as having an introduction to the role that they will be fulfilling. The benefit of this training is that:

- It allows an employee to understand what they need to do in their role. This helps to ensure that they become productive sooner. It also lets them know who their line manager is and where they fit into the structure.
- It helps a new employee to settle quickly so they feel confident, secure and less likely to leave. They will meet their colleagues, be shown how to login to computer systems, and be given a tour of the workplace, including canteens and changing areas.

Different training methods continued

On the job training

On the job training is usually conducted whilst the employee is undertaking their normal daily tasks. It is delivered by other, more experienced, members of staff.

Benefits
- Training can be tailored to the individual, and will meet the exact needs of the business.
- It is a cheaper way to train people.
- The individual is contributing whilst training.
- Training will involve all of the same systems, colleagues and types of equipment that are used within the business.

Drawbacks
- Unlikely to generate new ideas into the business.
- Having to train whilst undertaking a job you are not fully trained in can be stressful.
- Can take more employees away from their own work as they provide the training.
- Standards of customer service may fall until the training is complete.

Off the job training

Off the job training is training that staff attend away from their place of work, often in colleges or training centres.

Benefits
- Training is delivered by specialists.
- Usually highly structured and may provide the employee with a qualification.
- Can generate fresh ideas into a business.

Drawbacks
- Attending training courses can be expensive.
- Can take employees away from their work.
- Upskilled employees become more attractive to rival businesses offering higher pay.

Case study

Bella Cucina Bistro has three outlets and is known for its authentic Italian cuisine. The sudden departure of the Finance Manager left the management in a tight spot. The responsibility for managing accounts fell on the shoulders of Marco Rossi, a senior staff member, with no previous accounts experience except what he had learned as part of his Business degree. The management also had to organise the training of new wait staff to work in the newly opened third bistro. Sofia Bianchi, an experienced shift manager, was tasked with sorting out the training for these employees.

In the exam you may have to recommend which type of training is suitable in the circumstances laid out in the case study. Think what would be appropriate, for example off the job training for Marco would be best so that he could complete an Accounts qualification, whereas the new wait staff would benefit from on-the-job training where they could shadow the experienced shift manager.

OCR GCSE **Business**

3.6

STAFF DEVELOPMENT

Developing an employee not only benefits the individual but also has its advantages for the business. Staff can undertake training courses over a long period of time. These can include vocational and academic qualifications as well as apprenticeships.

Methods of staff development

Businesses can implement a staff development programme. These can either be vocational or academic.

- **Vocational** – Learning practical skills and techniques that are directly relevant for a particular occupation. It often involves becoming professionally certified in that area.
- **Academic** – Courses usually takes place away from an employee's usual place of work and involve learning theoretical knowledge about a particular topic. Examples include A Levels, Degrees and Master's Degrees.

A lot of businesses will offer apprenticeships. These are government backed schemes where the employee will conduct a mixture of on-the-job and off-the-job training.

Explain **one** benefit to a business of offering apprenticeships as a method of staff development. [2]

By offering apprenticeships, a business can obtain government funding,[1] therefore reducing business costs.[1] Training is tailored to the needs of the business[1] which aids accuracy, quality and productivity.[1] Apprentices are commonly loyal and stay on with a permanent role in the business[1] which improves staff retention and staff experience.[1]

The benefits to employees and businesses of staff development

Benefits to employees

- Gain qualifications and new skills.
- More likely to be awarded a promotion.
- Employees are paid whilst undertaking development.
- Businesses will pay for qualifications

Benefits to business

- Staff become more motivated.
- Retention is likely to be higher.
- Can help to fulfil skills shortages.
- Can help build a reputation for caring for employees, which helps with recruitment.

3.7

EMPLOYMENT LAW

Employment law governs how businesses interact and deal with their workers. Legislation will have an impact on recruitment and employment.

Employment law

Employment legislation is enforced in order to protect workers. Various laws are in place to stop employees from being exploited by their employers. It covers the following areas:

Recruitment

Businesses must ensure that employees have a legal right to work in the UK. This involves completing checks on new employees.

Pay

All employees are entitled to receive a minimum wage. Workers aged over 25 years old and above are entitled to receive the National Living Wage, which is slightly more than the National Minimum Wage.

Discrimination

The Equality Act (2010) brought together legislation which states that a business must not be discriminatory against employees. This includes discrimination on the basis of age, gender, race, religion, sexual orientation or because of disability. The business must ensure that they pay people the same amount of money for the same work completed.

Explain **one** impact on a business that does not comply with employment law. [2]

If a business pays its workers below the National Minimum Wage they are likely to be fined,[1] which will decrease the business' profits / reputation.[1]

Contracts

Employees have a right to be given a contract of employment. Contained within that contract will be the following information:

- Details of pay.
- Hours worked (normally employees cannot be asked to work more than 48 hours per week).
- Holiday entitlement.

Topic 3

CASE STUDY

Francisco Ravenelli founded Ravenelli Design Solutions in London during the 1980s, starting as a modest venture in a rapidly evolving industry. The business initially focused on traditional print-based materials, including brochures, but quickly expanded to include digital media services, such as designing and building websites. Over the decades, Francisco's dedication to quality and innovation transformed the agency into a well-respected entity, renowned for producing high-quality communications and branding material. Today, Ravenelli Design Solutions boasts a diverse portfolio with clients spanning the globe, each drawn to the agency's reputation for excellence and attention to detail.

Ravenelli Design Solutions operates with a flat structure, empowering designers by delegating significant responsibility to them. This approach fosters creativity and innovation, essential in the design industry. The organisation is structured by function, keeping the creative team separate from the sales team to ensure each can focus on their specialised tasks. Recognising the value of his staff, Francisco has implemented flexible working arrangements, including the option for designers to work from home. This flexibility not only attracts top talent from around the world but also enhances job satisfaction and productivity. Digital communication tools play a crucial role in the agency's operations, facilitating seamless interactions with international clients to understand their unique needs and deliver customised design solutions.

Recently, the retirement of the long-serving sales manager marked a significant transition for Ravenelli Design Solutions. Francisco and his board of directors are contemplating promoting from within the sales team to fill the vacancy, reflecting their belief in rewarding and developing existing talent. To retain top-tier designers, the agency offers competitive salaries, performance-based bonuses (based on the business' financial performance), and invests in employee development through industry-specific training programs. Francisco is also committed to nurturing new talent, offering annual apprenticeships to young individuals starting out in the design field. New employees are trained on the agency's bespoke software by existing colleagues, ensuring a smooth integration and upholding the high standards Ravenelli Design Solutions is known for. This comprehensive approach to staff development and retention underpins Francisco's philosophy that investing in people is key to sustaining the agency's legacy of excellence.

Topic 3

EXAMINATION PRACTICE

1. The manager of a supermarket uses on-the-job training to train employees. Which **one** of the following is a disadvantage of using on-the-job training to train new till workers? [1]
   A – It may take longer for shoppers to get their groceries scanned through the till
   B – It will cost the business more than sending them on external training courses
   C – No groceries can be sold while the training takes place
   D – The cashiers will be trained on different equipment to what they will use

2. Which **one** of the following is typically included in a contract of employment? [1]
   A – The company's annual profit
   B – The company's marketing strategy
   C – The employee's salary and benefits
   D – The number of customers the business serves

3. Identify **two** financial methods of motivation. [2]

4. Explain **one** reason why a business will produce a person specification. [2]

5. Explain **one** reason why it is important to have motivated employees. [2]

6. Explain **one** benefit of internal recruitment to a business. [2]

For the following questions, you must refer to the case study on the previous page.

7. Identify **two** items that may be included in induction training for Ravenelli Design Solutions. [2]

8. Explain **one** reason why digital communication is important to Ravenelli Design Solutions. [2]

9. Explain **one** benefit to Ravenelli Design Solutions from having a flat organisational structure. [2]

10. Analyse **one** benefit to Ravenelli Design Solutions of allowing workers to work from home. [3]

11. Ravenelli Design Solutions are considering using interviews and group activities in their recruitment.
    (a) Analyse **one** way that Ravenelli Design Solutions could use each of the following methods when selecting new employees:
        (i) Interviews [3]
        (ii) Group activities [3]
    (b) Recommend whether interviews or group activities are the best selection method for Ravenelli Design Solutions when selecting new employees. [3]

12. Evaluate whether Ravenelli Design Solutions should continue to offer apprenticeships. [9]

OCR GCSE **Business**

TOPICS FOR PAPER 2
Operations, finance and influences on business

Information about the paper

Specification coverage

Operations, finance, influences on business, and the interdependent nature of business

The content for this assessment will be drawn from the essential subject content sections 4 to 7 in the specification.

Assessment

Written exam: 1 hour 30 minutes

80 marks

All questions are mandatory

50% of the qualification grade

Calculators are permitted in this examination.

Assessment overview

The paper is divided into two sections:

Section A: 15 marks

Section B: 65 marks

The paper will consist of calculations, multiple-choice, short-answer and extended-writing questions.

Questions in Sections B will be based on business contexts given in the paper.

4.1

PRODUCTION PROCESSES

It is the purpose of the operations function within a business to produce goods and provide services to the customers. Products can be produced in a variety of ways and a business must choose which method is most suitable for them.

Methods of production

Job production

Job production involves the manufacture of a single, unique product to meet an individual order.

An example of this would be the construction of a sports stadium or the making of a bespoke wedding dress.

Batch production

Batch production is used to make sets of identical products in batches. Once one batch has been produced, modifications are made to the production process so that a batch of different products can be produced. Examples include the production of bread or furniture.

Flow production

Flow production (also known as mass production) involves the assembly of goods along a production line, often using robotics. Products will be identical and manufactured continuously in large quantities. Examples include the production of chocolate bars and glass bottles.

Method	Benefit	Drawback
Job	• Meets customers' exact requirements. • High profit margins. • Usually high quality.	• High unit costs, so a high price is set. • Skilled workforce required. • Can take longer to produce, so productivity is low.
Batch	• Faster than job production so it has higher productivity than job production. • Possible to use more machinery or automation compared to job production. • Some flexibility as modifications to the process can be made.	• Time is needed to make modifications between batches, therefore it is slower than flow. • Greater cost per item than flow production. • Less opportunity to make specialised products for customers.
Flow	• Low average unit costs. • Fast / high production. • Use of robotics allows for 24/7 manufacture.	• Expensive to set up due to the cost of machinery. • Repetitive work is demotivating for workers. • A breakdown on the production line halts all production.

OCR GCSE **Business**

4.1

INFLUENCE OF TECHNOLOGY ON PRODUCTION

Technology is increasingly used in the production of goods and services. Many businesses will take advantage of automation, robotics and computers to gain a productive advantage.

Use of technology in the production process

Automation

Many processes and business workflow, such as payment systems, payroll, stock control or analytics, could be streamlined using software systems and technology.

Computers

Technology has enabled modifications in design and production much more easily through the use of **Computer Aided Design** (**CAD**) and **Computer Aided Manufacture** (**CAM**).

Robotics

Robots are machines that are programmed to perform a certain task whilst employed on a production line. A business could install automated technology on a production line, replacing workers with technology, which is used to manufacturer a product.

Benefits of technology in production	Drawbacks of technology in production
⊕ Replaces workers, which commonly reduces costs and increases output.	⊖ May need to train workers in the use and maintenance of technology.
⊕ Productivity is increased as production lines can be operational 24/7 without breaks.	⊖ Initial cost of purchasing technology can be expensive.
⊕ Waste is reduced as technology is often more accurate than humans.	⊖ Machines can breakdown, often severely impacting productivity.

Explain **one** way that technology has impacted on the quality of a business' product. [2]

One way is that consistently identical products are produced.[1] This is because robotics can manufacture products with extreme precision and exact specifications.[1]

4.2

THE CONCEPT OF QUALITY

A business' goods and services must be of a sufficient standard to satisfy customers' needs and wants. If quality falls short of these expectations, then the business could suffer as a result.

A quality product or service means that:
- The product is fit for purpose.
- The product does everything that the customer expects.
- The product meets all safety and legal requirements.

Methods of ensuring quality

Quality control

Quality control involves checking the quality of a product at the end of the production line by a team of quality controllers and inspectors. Their job is to ensure that each product or batch meets a specific set of standards before being sold to customers.

Benefits

- Defective products will not make it to market.
- The system is not disruptive to workers as quality is inspected at the end of production.

> Explain **one** drawback to a business from implementing a quality control system. [2]
>
> *One way is that there can be a lot of wasted products,[1] because defects are only found at the end of a production process.[1] A quality control process can be costly,[1] because inspectors must be paid.[1]*

Quality assurance

Quality assurance requires each individual worker to be responsible for the quality of their own work.

Quality is a focus at every stage of the production process. As such it aims to prevent errors from being made in the first place.

Benefits

- Can be motivating to staff as they have more responsibility.
- In theory there should be no wastage as errors are rectified immediately before the products move along a production line.

> Explain **one** drawback to a business from implementing a quality assurance system. [2]
>
> *Production may be more time consuming.[1] This is because each worker checks their own work.[1] Staff may need more training,[1] because they will have extra responsibility.[1]*

OCR GCSE **Business**

4.2

THE IMPORTANCE OF QUALITY

A business should maintain a high standard of quality when manufacturing goods or providing a service as there are many benefits in doing so. The consequences of not maintaining quality can be catastrophic for a business.

Benefits of having a high-quality product

Improves the reputation of the business – By producing a high-quality product, consumers will spread positive messages about the business.

It avoids waste – If care is taken as the product is produced, then waste can be kept to a minimum, further reducing costs.

Satisfy customer needs and returning customers – If goods or services meet customers' expectations, then they are more likely to return to make repeat purchases.

To gain new customers – If potential customers read good reviews and hear positive reports about a brand, then they may be more inclined to make a purchase.

Reduced product returns and recalls – If product quality is high and it does as a customer expects, then returns will be limited. Not only does this further add to reputational benefits but helps to lower the costs of warehousing, distribution and administration.

Allows a higher price to be charged – Customers will be more willing to pay a higher price if they know they are going to receive a better-quality product or service in return.

Explain **one** risk to a business from producing a product that does not meet customer expectations. [2]

One risk is that the business may suffer reputational damage.[1] This can lead to negative word of mouth affecting future sales.[1] Other responses could include: customer complaints, an increase in the number of returned products, or a loss of customers.

4.3

METHODS OF SELLING

There are three methods of selling and these can be used to sell both goods and services, and to sell to consumers and other businesses. The most appropriate methods will depend on a number of factors.

Face-to face selling

Face-to-face selling involves a meeting in person between the buyer and seller. This method can help a business increase sales as customers can get advice and a more personal service. For some businesses, face-to-face is unavoidable, for example a restaurant. However, it is not always convenient for a customer to visit a business and the costs to a retailer of setting up a physical location can be very high.

Telesales

Some business will sell products over the telephone. A business may contact potential customers directly in an attempt to persuade them to buy their products. A benefit of this method is that it is cheaper than selling through a retail outlet. Customers also get the chance to ask questions, which can then lead to increased sales.

> Explain **one** disadvantage to a business from conducting telesales. [1]
>
> *Customers may find telesales calls annoying.[1] Therefore the business gets a negative reputation as a result.[1] Alternative answers include: costs involved in storing goods in a warehouse and paying telesales staff.*

E-commerce

E-commerce is the buying and selling of goods and services over the internet. It also allows customers to make purchases at any time of day and at their own convenience, whilst allowing a business to reach a much wider target market.

Benefits

- Can reach new markets, including overseas.
- Can keep costs low by not having an expensive physical location.
- Can sell more products as businesses are not restricted by physical opening hours.
- More convenient for customers as they can order from home, leading to more sales.

Drawbacks

- Customers can easily make price comparisons, putting pressure on businesses to have low prices.
- Businesses will have to pay to distribute products to customers, or pass this cost onto them, making purchases more expensive.
- As customers cannot physically see or try on products, there may be high levels of returns.
- Businesses will have to make sure that their websites are secure so customers' personal details are not stolen.

OCR GCSE **Business**

4.3

CUSTOMER SERVICE

Offering good customer service is one way that a business can gain an advantage over competitors. By looking after customers, a business will gain a good reputation that will help them to be successful.

Benefits of good customer service

- Reputational benefits
- Increased customer satisfaction
- Customers purchase more products
- Source of added value
- **Good customer service**
- Greater chance of making profit
- Source of competitive advantage
- Customers become loyal

1. Analyse **one** benefit to a business of providing good customer service. [3]

   Good customer service will lead to satisfied and loyal customers as they feel that the business really values them.[1] As a result, they are more likely to make repeat purchases,[1] / leave favourable online reviews of their experience,[1] which could lead to an increase in reputation,[1] / potentially a growth in sales and revenue for the business.[1]

After-sales service

An after-sales service is provided to customers after they have bought a product. It includes providing further advice or technical support, as well as dealing with returns if the customer is not satisfied. Providing good after-sales service helps increase customer confidence in the business, enhancing reputation and future sales.

2. Explain **one** drawback to a business from providing an after-sales service. [2]

   The business may have to train workers in order to provide this service,[1] therefore the businesses costs may increase.[1]

The sales process

Good service throughout the sales process involves the following:

Product knowledge

Being able to answer customers' questions will help them determine which good or service is most suitable for fulfilling their needs. It will make a customer feel more confident when purchasing from a business that really understands what it offers.

- There will be increased trust from consumers because employees can provide help, advice and suggestions.
- The business is more likely to receive good reviews.
- Employees will be more confident and independent so may be more motivated.

Providing good customer service isn't cheap. To ensure that employees possess good product knowledge and know how to engage with customers positively, they will need to be fully trained. This can increase the costs to a business.

Customer engagement

Any interaction between the customer and the business should be positive in order to make people want to engage with the business more. Making the customer feel valued will enhance their experience and ensure that they know that the business cares about them.

Even a complaint can be turned into a positive experience if it is handled really well in an efficient, understanding and knowledgeable way.

3. Explain **one** benefit to a business when staff positively engage with customers. [2]

   It will make a customer feel more comfortable with the buying experience,[1] therefore they are more likely to make a purchase, increasing the business' sales.[1]

OCR GCSE **Business**

4.4

CONSUMER LAW

There are various pieces of **legislation** that govern how businesses behave. Consumer law ensures that buyers are protected from being exploited by businesses.

Consumer law

Consumer law is enforced to ensure that consumers are protected from malpractice by businesses. The Consumer Rights Act (2015) protects consumers by addressing the quality of products and the rights of the consumer by stating that:

- Products should work properly and be fit for purpose.
- Products must be **safe** to use and of **satisfactory quality**.
- Products must be as described.
- Consumers have the right to return unsuitable products within a period of 30 days.
- The business is responsible for its goods until the customer has taken possession of them.
- The business must repair or replace faulty products or refund the customer.

Consumers have the legal right to their money back, or to have their product repaired or replaced if the business does not meet these principles.

A product recall may be made by a manufacturer where it identifies an issue. All customers are then entitled to return their goods for repair or replacement at no cost.

Recent examples include a supermarket recall of hummus owing to salmonella fears, and a car manufacturer recalling vehicles for checks on faulty curtain airbags.

Explain **one** consequence to a business of not complying with consumer law. [2]

One consequence could be that the business could be fined.[1] This would add to the costs of the business making it harder to break-even.[1] Alternative answers could include: reputational damage[1] and loss of sales.[1]

⭐ In the exam you may have to apply the principles of consumer law to a particular business. For instance, an example could be a question about a plumbing business that has installed an electric shower. The question could ask you about how that plumbing business will meet consumer law. In this instance, you could say that they must supply a shower that meets current safety standards.

62 ClearRevise

4.5

BUSINESS LOCATION

The location that a business chooses can have a huge impact on its success. There are various factors that will determine which location is best. These vary in importance depending on the nature of the business.

Factors influencing the location decision of a business

Labour: Businesses need sufficient available workers close by who have the required skills. A business needs to locate close to where people are willing and able to work.

Costs: Not all businesses can afford to locate wherever they want. The cost of the most sought-after locations will be more expensive. Therefore, a business on a budget may choose a location based on cost.

Availability of raw materials: Some businesses may require large bulky raw materials, such as timber, to be able to produce their product. Transporting the supplies to the business may be expensive so, to keep costs down, businesses may choose to locate close to the raw materials they need.

Proximity to market: For some businesses, being close to their customers will be the most important factor. By doing this, it can raise awareness of the business and help it to become established. This is particularly important for retail businesses.

OCR GCSE **Business**

63

4.6
WORKING WITH SUPPLIERS

Procurement is the term used to describe the process a business goes through in finding and obtaining the right materials and supplies to be used in the production process.

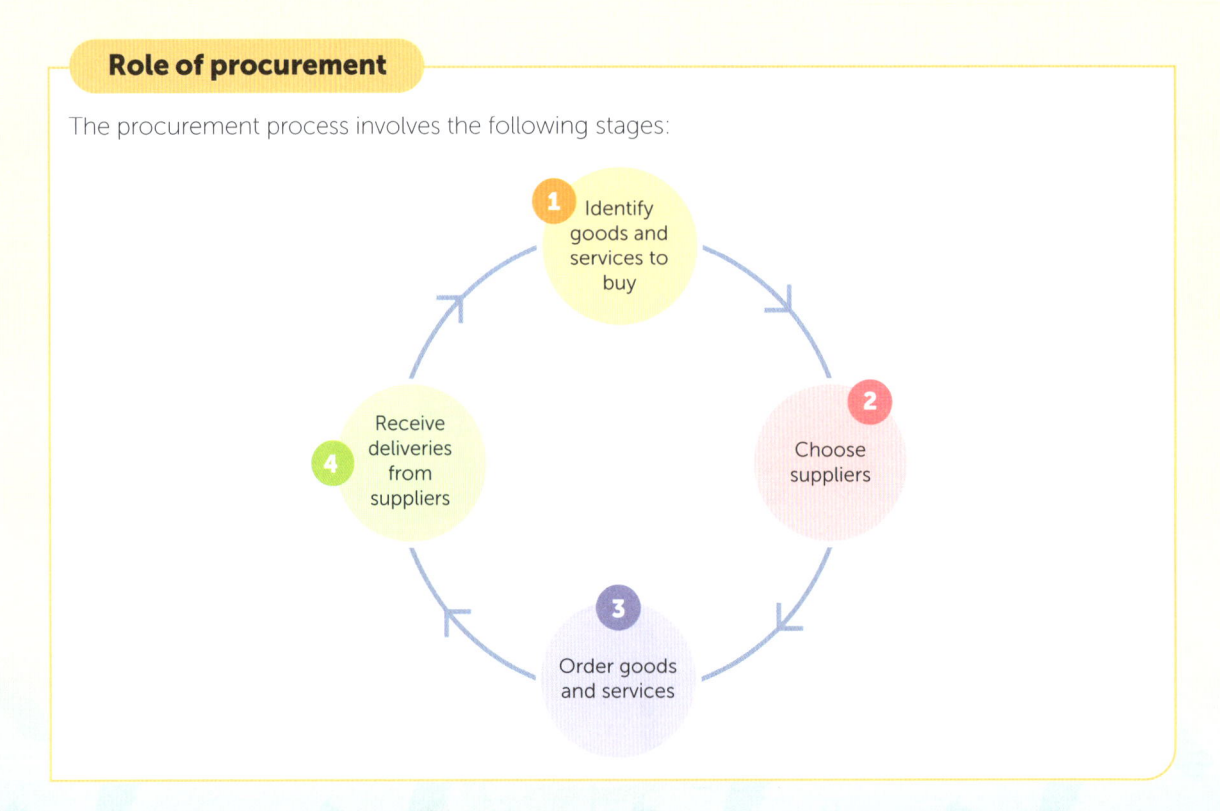

Role of procurement

The procurement process involves the following stages:

1. Identify goods and services to buy
2. Choose suppliers
3. Order goods and services
4. Receive deliveries from suppliers

Factors affecting the choice of suppliers

If a business can find the right supplier, the production process can become more efficient.

The right supplier:
- will supply the best **quality** materials at the best possible **price**.
- will negotiate their own prices so that trade customers can make cost savings, particularly when buying in bulk, or where there is a long-standing relationship.
- will be flexible, quick and **reliable** in delivery so that the business gets the right supplies, at the right time, avoiding stoppages in production or sales.
- has the materials that a business needs in stock.
- can be trusted.
- offers favourable payment terms.

Impact of logistical and supply decisions on businesses

Logistics refers to the management of supplies and finished products throughout the **supply chain**, in order to ensure that deliveries arrive on time for the production process. It is also concerned with ensuring that deliveries of finished goods to customers are timely.

Logistical issues

The following factors need to be considered when making logistical or supply chain decisions:

Time

The supplier must be able to deliver the goods on time. If they cannot, then this can cause delays in getting the product to the customer, which may create reputational damage. A business could lose sales or repeat business as a result.

Reliability

Suppliers must be able to deliver the products on time to their customers, and be able to deliver the right amount. The quality of the supplies must also be appropriate.

Costs

A business will want to keep costs to a minimum so it will be looking at keeping supply and delivery costs as low as possible, but this cannot be at the expense of quality or reliability.

Customer service

Just as a business will provide a high level of customer service to its customers, it will want a high level of service from its own suppliers.

Length of the supply chain

A long supply chain is one that contains a large number of businesses. If this is the case, then there is increased risk of problems occurring at any point in the chain increasing potential issues with obtaining the right supplies. If a component is missing, a business may not be able to proceed with the manufacture of its product.

Explain **two** impacts that effective procurement and logistics can have on a business. [4]

One impact is that the business can become more efficient.[1] This is because by having reliable logistics, delivery of materials to be used in production won't be late.[1]

Another impact is that the business could have lower unit costs,[1] because effective procurement will allow a business to negotiate better deals for its supplies.[1]

OCR GCSE **Business**

Topic 4

CASE STUDY

SweetDelights Ltd is a well-established factory specialising in the production of a variety of sweets. The manufacturer has recently introduced technology to the production process and now uses flow production to mass produce its sweets. The manufacturer has also introduced technology in how it sells its sweets. Traditionally, orders for sweets have been taken over the phone. Now SweetDelights has introduced online ordering, allowing confectionery retailers to purchase sweets at their own convenience.

With an increasing demand for their products, the company is facing a critical decision regarding the selection of a supplier for one of its key ingredients. SweetDelights relies on a specific ingredient, SugarX, to manufacture its signature sweets. Currently, the company has been sourcing SugarX from Supplier A for the past five years. However, due to changing market dynamics, SweetDelights is exploring the possibility of switching to Supplier B, which has recently entered the market with competitive pricing and claims of superior product quality.

SweetDelights Ltd has done some research on the two suppliers:

Costs	• Supplier A has been a reliable partner for several years, offering consistent quality at a reasonable price. • Supplier B, while relatively new, is offering a lower price for SugarX, creating the potential for cost savings.
Quality	• SweetDelights Ltd has built a reputation for high-quality sweets, and any compromise in the quality of SugarX may impact the final product. • Supplier B claims to have a more advanced production process, resulting in a higher quality SugarX.
Reliability and delivery time	• Supplier A has a proven track record of timely deliveries, ensuring that SweetDelights Ltd can meet customer demand consistently. • Supplier B is relatively untested in terms of reliability and may pose a risk in terms of meeting production schedules.
Relationship and loyalty	• SweetDelights Ltd values the long-standing relationship with Supplier A and acknowledges the importance of loyalty in business partnerships. • Shifting to Supplier B might strain relationships with Supplier A and could impact future collaborations.

The management at SweetDelights Ltd is faced with a challenging decision. The company must weigh up the benefits of cost savings and potential quality improvement against the risks of disrupting a longstanding relationship with Supplier A.

Topic 4

EXAMINATION PRACTICE

1. A customer goes to buy a new mobile phone from a shop in their local town. By law, the phone shop must: [1]
   A – Match the price charged by a competitor phone shop
   B – Offer to upgrade the phone at no extra cost
   C – Provide insurance for the phone to protect it from any damages
   D – Supply a phone of satisfactory quality

2. Which of the following is a benefit of automation? [1]
   A – Finance will be required as it is an initially expensive process
   B – Production can be disrupted if machines malfunction
   C – Productivity is likely to increase
   D – Workers may need to be re-trained

3. Explain **one** benefit to a business of implementing a system of quality control. [2]

4. Explain **one** reason why a business may choose to locate close to its market. [2]

5. Explain **one** benefit to a business of having effective procurement. [2]

For the following questions, you must refer to the case study on the previous page.

6. Analyse **one** benefit to SweetDelights Ltd from introducing an e-commerce system. [3]

7. Analyse **one** way in which SweetDelights Ltd can offer good customer service. [3]

8. Analyse **two** impacts on SweetDelights Ltd from using flow production. [6]

9. Analyse the importance of having a quality product to SweetDelights Ltd [3]

10. Evaluate whether SweetDelights Ltd should change to Supplier B. [9]

5.1 THE FINANCE FUNCTION

The finance function refers to the finance department and the activities and responsibilities of the people working in that department. It is larger businesses that will have a finance department, and this functional area will impact on the other areas; marketing, operations and people.

The purpose of the finance function

Providing financial information: There are lots of different pieces of financial information that a finance department may have to provide. These include details of:
- profit or loss made (including gross profit, net profit and the profitability ratios)
- cash flow (expected revenues and expenditures)
- break-even.

Arranging finance: Gaining finance from the bank in terms of loans or overdraft or arranging the issuing of shares. The finance function is responsible for anticipating periods where the business may be short of cash and resolving any issues.

Support business planning and decision making: The finance function allocates budgets and provides accurate financial information to managers so that they can make informed decisions about potential investments, or actions that they may be considering.

Managing finances: Making payments (wages and bills) whilst also managing the business' receipts from sales.

The influence of the finance function on business activity

The finance department will impact the other functional areas in a number of ways.

Functional area	How finance can influence functional area
Marketing	Finance departments will set promotional budgets. This may mean that the marketing function must alter how they will promote the product and may have to use different advertising methods.
Production	The finance department will calculate how much it costs to make a product. If it is particularly high, then the production department may have to find cheaper suppliers.
People	The finance function may provide information on the cost of employment to the Human Resources team. This may limit how much recruitment they can undertake.

5.2

WHY BUSINESSES NEED FINANCE

All businesses need finance, whether they are just starting-up or whether they are well established. Businesses first need to establish the reasons as to why they need finance. Then they can then assess the different sources available to them, in order to determine which is the most appropriate.

The reasons businesses need finance

Establishing a new business: A new start-up will need to buy things before it can begin to produce or sell anything. It may need to rent or buy premises as well as potentially needing to purchase equipment and furniture, all before buying tools and materials required to manufacture a good or to provide a service.

Funding expansion: As a business becomes established it may decide that it wants to scale up by producing and selling more goods. To do this it may have to purchase a larger factory, along with all the equipment and machinery needed. Service sector firms may require larger premises so that they can serve a greater number of customers. Some businesses will open locations in other parts of the country or overseas – all of these need financing.

Recruitment: Going through the recruitment process to find and select new employees is a cost to a business that needs financing. Whether they are employing additional people due to expansion, or recruiting to replace workers that have left, a business may need to pay to advertise the jobs and hold selection days.

To run the business: Finance is needed to keep a business running on a day-to-day basis. Businesses need to pay for materials from suppliers, pay expenses such as heating and lighting as well as paying the wages and salaries of their employees.

Other reasons for requiring finance may include managing cash flow, to cover costs, for refurbishment or to improve quality.

Explain **one** reason why marketing may require finance. [2]

The marketing department may require finance because promotional campaigns need to be funded.[1] This is because advertising on television, or via sponsorship will cost money.[1]

OCR GCSE **Business**

5.2

SOURCES OF FINANCE

There are many different sources that a business may use to raise finance. They can be classified as short-term or long-term as well as internal or external.

There are different factors that will determine which is best for a particular business.

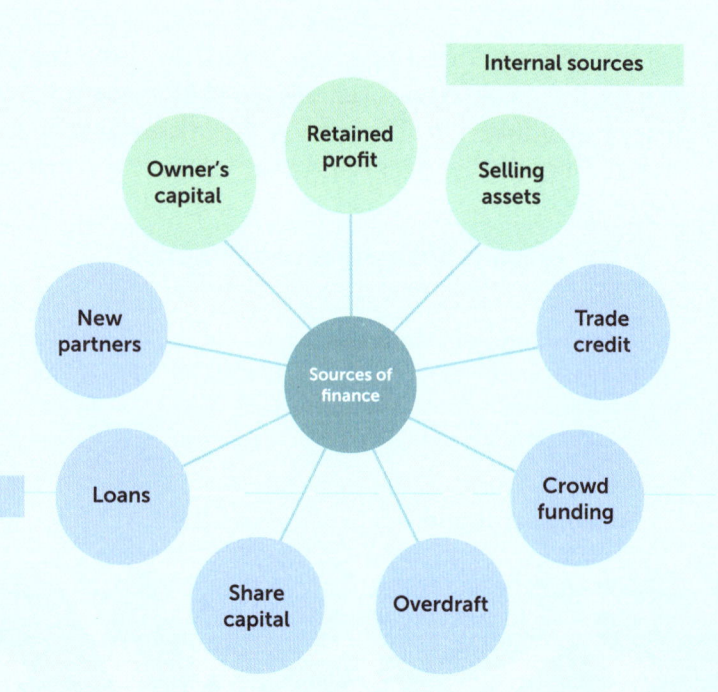

Internal sources: Owner's capital, Retained profit, Selling assets

External sources: New partners, Trade credit, Loans, Share capital, Overdraft, Crowd funding

Short-term sources

Overdraft

This is an agreement with a bank that allows a business to spend more than they have in their bank account. This must be repaid to the bank, usually with high interest. Businesses normally use this method to solve short-term cash flow issues.

Trade credit

Trade credit is offered when a business receives goods from a supplier but doesn't actually pay for them until after an agreed amount of time (e.g. 28 days).

> **How to suggest the most suitable source of finance:**
>
> In the exam you may have to recommend which source of finance may be most suitable for the business that is presented in the case study relating to the question. This may be influenced by a number of factors, including whether it's a new business or not. Clearly a new business will not be able to use retained profit whereas an established business will.
>
> Other factors such as the legal structure will impact the choice. Limited companies can issue shares to raise money whereas a sole trader or partnership cannot.
>
> Look to see what circumstances the business in the case study is facing and use the information provided to help make your recommendation!

Long-term sources

Retained profit can also be used as a short term source of finance.

Retained profit

Profit that a business has already generated can be reinvested. This is cheaper than other sources and it allows the owners to maintain their control. However, once it is used, the business will not be able to use it for other projects. Whether it is suitable may depend on how much profit the business generates.

Owner's capital

The owners of sole traders and partnerships may choose to invest their own funds into the business. A benefit of this is that it does not need to be repaid, but it does mean that the owner won't have the funds available for anything else. If a business owner doesn't have any savings, they may also obtain the finance from friends and family. A business may invite new owners or partners to invest their money.

Share capital

Share capital is finance raised by issuing or selling shares in a business. One benefit is that large amounts of funds can be sourced, while also keeping ongoing costs to a minimum as no repayments are made. However, depending on how many shares are given away, it could mean that the owners lose control.

New partner

Bringing a new partner into a business can inject new ideas and some additional income, often through investment or the sale of shares to the new partner.

Loans

A business can borrow money from a bank, receiving a large lump sum. They will make monthly repayments back to the bank, which will include interest. A **mortgage** is a specific loan for purchasing property. Whether this is suitable may depend on how high the interest rate is and how much of a risk the bank thinks the business is.

Selling assets

Assets can include machinery, buildings or intellectual property. Raising funds in this way is cheap as no repayments are necessary. The drawback of this option is that once sold, the business will not be able to use the assets. Whether selling assets is appropriate may be dependent on how much the assets are required.

Crowd funding

This involves a business making an online appeal to investors who each invest small amounts of money, in order to raise a large amount overall. If the target amount of finance is not reached, the business does not get the money and their reputation may be harmed.

OCR GCSE **Business**

5.3

REVENUE, COSTS, PROFIT AND LOSS

To be able to accurately calculate **profit**, a business will need to know its **revenue** and its **total costs**. If a business can calculate these, then it can also analyse what profit it will make at different sales levels.

Revenue

Revenue is also referred to as **sales revenue**. It is the total amount of income made from selling a good or service. It is calculated by using the following formula:

Revenue = selling price × number of units sold

Fixed and variable costs

Fixed

Fixed costs are those that do not change in line with changes in output. An example would be advertising costs.

Variable costs

Variable costs are those that will change directly with changes in output. An example would be raw materials. The formula for total variable costs is:

Total variable costs = variable cost per unit × number of units sold

Total costs

Total costs are all the costs added together that a business incurs in making a product or providing a service.

Total costs = fixed costs + variable costs

Profit

Profit is made when the revenue received exceeds the total costs. If a business has total costs that are greater than revenue it is called a **loss**.

Profit = revenue − total costs

1. Remi makes homemade chocolates and sells them at local food fayres and in shops around her area. She has provided the following information:
   - Average selling price of a box of chocolates - £5.50
   - Fixed costs of running the business - £12,500
   - Variable cost for each box of chocolates - £2.00

   Calculate the profit made if Remi sells 5000 boxes. [4]

   Revenue = 5.50 × 5,000 = £27,500[1]
   Total Variable cost = 2.00 × 5,000 = £10,000[1]
   Total costs = FC + VC = 12,500 + 10,000 = 22,500[1]
   Profit = Revenue − Total costs = 27,500 − 22,500 = £5,000[1]

Calculating gross and net profit

There are different measures of profit that a business needs to calculate in order to assess their performance. These are gross profit and net profit. However, to fully assess profitability a business will also need to calculate and interpret profit margins.

Gross profit

Gross profit is the difference between a business' revenue and the costs associated with making the product, known as the **cost of sales**. Cost of sales includes items such as the cost of raw materials.

Gross profit = revenue − cost of sales

Net profit

Net profit is the difference between gross profit and operating expenses. Included in operating expenses are the fixed costs not directly associated with making the product. They also include any interest that the business owes on finance borrowed.

Net profit =
gross profit − other operating expenses and interest

Corey Wade
DESIGN & SCULPTURE, DONCASTER

	£
Revenue	95,450
− Cost of sales	39,850
= Gross profit	55,600
− Other operating expenses and interest	41,500
= Net profit	14,100

Gross and net profit margin

> Gross profit margin = (Gross profit ÷ revenue) × 100
> Net profit margin = (Net profit ÷ revenue) × 100

The **gross profit margin** is a measure of how profitable a business is at making and selling a good or service. The **net profit margin** is a test of the overall profitability of the business after it considers all the expenses of the business.

A gross profit of 58.25% means that for every £100 of revenue £58.25 of it is gross profit. A net profit margin of 14.77% means that there is £14.77 of net profit in every £100 of revenue. To assess how a business has performed, it needs to compare these figures with those from recent years and with those of competitor firms.

---

2. Using the Income Statement for Corey Wade, calculate, to two decimal places:
   (a) The gross profit margin [2]
   (b) The net profit margin [2]

(a) GPM = (55,600 ÷ 95,450) × 100 = 58.25%
(b) NPM = (14,100 ÷ 95,450) × 100 = 14.77%

OCR GCSE **Business**

5.3
AVERAGE RATE OF RETURN

A business must often choose between different investment opportunities. For instance, it could have to decide whether to purchase new machinery for its factory or to upgrade its delivery vans. Management will use the average rate of return to help decide which is best.

Investment projects that businesses undertake

Businesses will invest in new assets. They will use these assets to help produce goods and provide services. The main categories that businesses will invest in are:

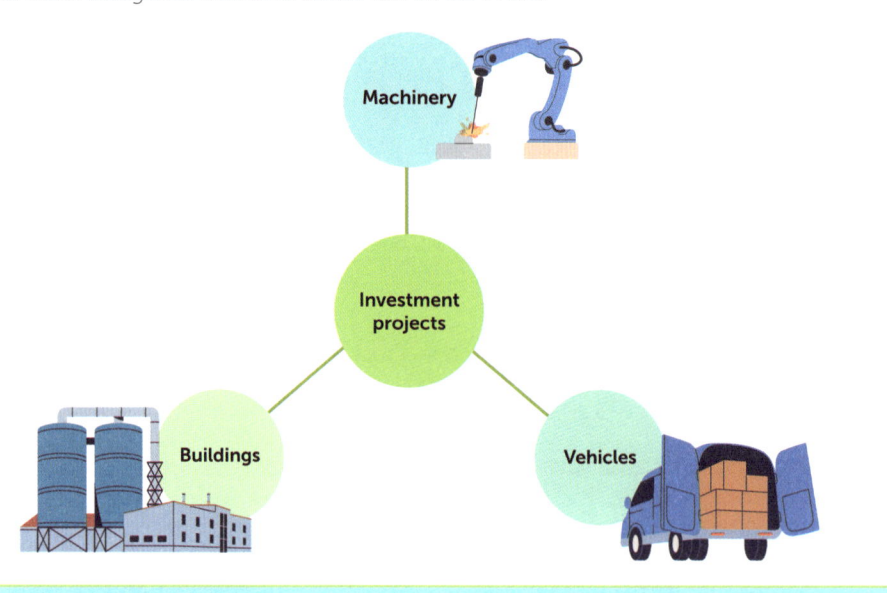

- Machinery
- Buildings
- Vehicles

(Investment projects)

Average rate of return

Before deciding which investment project to commit to, a business will calculate the **average rate of return** (**ARR**) of different investment projects in order to easily compare the financial merit of each option. ARR is a calculation that allows a business to work out the average yearly profit, as a percentage, on an investment.

Calculating average rate of return

To calculate the average rate of return (ARR) of a project, a business will use the following formula:

ARR = (Average return per annum ÷ initial sum invested) × 100

You may have to calculate the average return per annum first before applying the formula.

A farming collective has the opportunity to invest in a new range of machinery. The cost of purchasing the vehicles is £36m. Over the next 6 years, it is anticipated they could generate an additional £54m of profit. Calculate the average rate of return if the farming collective were to invest in the new technology. Show your working. [4]

Average return per annum = £54m ÷ 6 years[1] = £9m per year.[1]
Average rate of return = (£9m ÷ £36) × 100[1] = 25%[1]

⭐ The question in the exam may ask you to give your answer to 1 or 2 decimal places. If this is the case make sure you follow the instructions so as not to lose marks.

Interpreting ARR

Average rate of return is a measure of profitability, so the higher the result the better. The agricultural collective in the question above has the opportunity to invest in an additional fleet of machinery, and if it does, the predicted ARR is 25%. This means that for every £100 invested in the project, it will yield a yearly profit of £25.

If the agricultural collective had a choice of investment projects to invest in, then it would, on financial grounds alone, select the investment with the highest percentage rate of return.

OCR GCSE **Business**

5.4

BREAK-EVEN

A company will **break even** when it sells enough products to generate sufficient revenue to cover its total costs.

Break-even

A business will break even point when the revenue it receives from selling its products, is equal to the amount that it costs to produce that good or provide that service.

Calculating break-even

A new business must know how much it needs to sell so that it can ensure that the business is viable. A break-even analysis is used to aid a business in making decisions about what price to charge, how much to produce and to help in managing costs.

It can be calculated using this formula:

Break-even =
fixed costs ÷ (selling price − variable cost per unit)

Interpreting a break-even chart

Businesses can use a break-even chart to find out the following information:

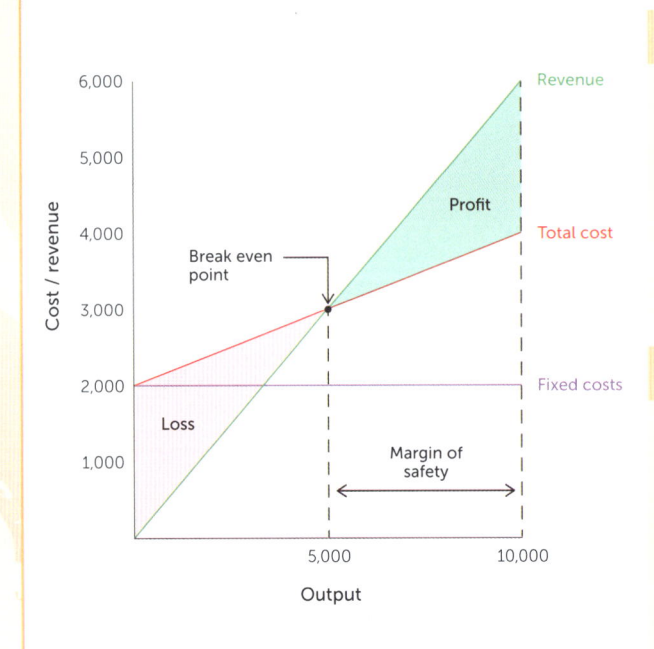

Break-even point

This is also known as the **break-even level of output**. As you can see in the chart opposite, this particular business needs to sell 5,000 products in order to receive enough revenue to cover its total costs. At this point, profit would be £0; neither a profit nor a loss is made.

Profit (loss)

Beyond the break-even point, revenue exceeds total costs. Therefore, the business is making a profit at any output level above 5,000. Below the break-even level of output, total costs are greater than revenue, so the business is making a loss.

Margin of safety

The **margin of safety** is the difference between the actual output of a business and the break-even level of output. If the business in the chart above is producing 10,000 units, then the margin of safety will be 5,000 units (10,000 − 5,000). This means that sales can drop by 5,000 units before the business becomes unprofitable.

Usefulness of break-even in business decision-making

Break-even analysis informs **marketing** and **planning** decisions.

Advantages of break-even

Break-even analysis is particularly useful for new start-up businesses as it will allow them to see if their business is viable. This is because they will know how many products they need to sell to cover their costs and can then decide whether that is an achievable amount.

Break-even is used for 'what-if' analysis. A business can change the variables such as the selling price and variable cost per unit, to see what impact that has on the level of break-even. This will also tell decision makers what might happen to profit levels, so they can create a strategy related to price, production levels and costs.

It also forms an important part of the financial planning section of a business plan. An entrepreneur can show potential investors the level of output they need to break-even. As a result, that investor, whether it be the bank or someone else, can make an informed decision as to whether they will provide the required finance to the business.

Disadvantages of break-even

1. Identify and explain **two** disadvantages to a business of using break-even analysis. [4]

   Break-even assumes all products are sold.[1] In reality, some products will be made but left unsold, which would mean a higher break-even point than if they had been sold.[1]

   Variable costs per unit are assumed to remain the same.[1] This is not usually the case because a business buying in bulk from a supplier will often receive a discount, which would make the break-even point lower.[1]

   Prices of raw materials may also change over time as new stock is ordered[1] which could alter the break-even point.[1]

   Break-even assumes that every product is sold at the same price point.[1] An increase in sales price would create a lower break-even point / could cause lower sales.[1]

2. Reanna runs a dog grooming business. She charges £30 per hour. Her fixed costs of running her business are £36 000. Her variable costs are £4 per hour.

   How many hours of dog grooming will Reanna need to do to start making a profit?

   A: 1059   B: 1385   C: 2340   D: 3060   [1]

   B: 1385.
   Break-even = 36 000 ÷ (30 − 4) = 1384.615.
   Round up to nearest hour = 1385

OCR GCSE **Business**

5.5

CASH-FLOW

Cash flow is the amount of money flowing into and out of a business over a period of time. Having enough cash is critical to a business. Many businesses fail because they do not have sufficient cash to pay all their bills.

The importance of cash to a business

A business uses cash to pay for all its day-to-day expenses. This includes paying for its supplies and wages for its employees. Without their help, most businesses could not continue. Without supplies, a business could not produce its product or provide its service.

If a business does not have enough cash to pay for its bills when they are due, it is said to be **insolvent**. This will lead to the failure of the business.

Difference between cash and profit

Cash is the amount of money that a business has available to pay for its day-to-day expenses. **Profit** is the difference between revenue and total costs. (See **pages 72**.) A profitable business can run out of cash. This is because a business records revenue as soon as a sale is made, but they may not receive actual payment immediately. In the interim period, large bills may become due, causing cash flow problems.

---

1. Identify and explain **two** reasons why a business might run out of cash. [4]

1. A business might experience seasonal sales.[1] This means that at certain times in the year they may have very little cash flowing into the business as they are not selling anything.[1]

   There may be an unexpected rise in costs, for example the price of raw materials.[1] This would increase cash outflows, meaning a lower than expected closing balance every month.[1]

   Other reasons include: poor credit terms from suppliers; having too much cash tied up in stock that hasn't sold; unexpected changes in demand; overtrading (spending too much on expansion).

Usefulness of cash flow forecasting

Planning or targeting tool: By forecasting cash flow, a business will know if it has liquidity, meaning it can afford to pay all its bills. It is also used as part of the business planning process; a bank manager would be able to see if they have enough cash to make repayments on a loan.

Anticipating periods of cash shortages: A cash flow forecast will show if there are months where a business does not have enough cash to cover for all the things it has to pay for.

Enables remedies to be put in place for shortages: If the cash flow forecast informs a manager that they will be short of cash for a short-time period, they can arrange an overdraft with their bank to cover this period, or they could negotiate better credit terms with their suppliers. They could also think about where else they could cut expenditure.

Interpreting cash flow forecasts

A **cash flow forecast** is a prediction of future cash inflows and outflows for a business. Below is an example:

£	Jan	Feb	Mar	Apr
Total receipts	110,000	90,000	70,000	80,000
Total payments	75,000	135,000	95,000	60,000
Net cash flow	35,000	(45,000)	(25,000)	20,000
Opening balance	25,000	60,000	15,000	(10,000)
Closing balance	60,000	15,000	(10,000)	10,000

A business will use a forecast to spot, in advance, when it is likely to have cash flow difficulties. Therefore, the business can take action to ensure that it does not run out of cash. In the example above, the business looks like it will have problems in March.

> A short-term loan, overdraft, request for additional trade credit or re-scheduling payments may resolve the cash flow problem presented here.

⭐ Remember the following formulae. An exam question could ask you to fill in the blanks on a cash-flow forecast, but you won't have to create a complete forecast.
- Net cash flow = total receipts − total payments
- Closing balance = opening balance + net cash flow
- Opening balance is always the same as the previous month's closing balance

---

2. Look at the following extract from a cash flow forecast:

	January	February
Total cash inflows	13,425	13,700
Total cash outflows	14,650	13,750
Net cash flow	(1,225)	(50)
Opening balance	12,000	
Closing balance	10,775	

Calculate the closing balance for February. [2]

2. February opening balance = 12,000 − 1225 = 10,775 or same as January closing balance[1]
February closing balance = 10,775 − 50 = £10,725[1]

OCR GCSE **Business**

Topic 5

CASE STUDY 5

As a leading online television entertainment company, StreamFlix PLC has revolutionised the way audiences consume their favourite movies, TV series, and sports content. Operating on a subscription-based model, StreamFlix offers subscribers access to a vast library of the latest blockbuster releases and television shows. Beyond traditional entertainment offerings, StreamFlix distinguishes itself with excellent sports coverage, showcasing a diverse range of live events from around the globe, catering to all the interests of its subscribers.

With a strategy to continue expanding its sports portfolio, StreamFlix is contemplating a bid for the rights to broadcast the next international women's football tournament. However, the substantial cost of £500 million for global rights presents a formidable financial challenge. To finance this ambitious project, StreamFlix must consider options such as borrowing capital or issuing additional shares. The decision to pursue this investment hinges on its potential to enhance the platform's value proposition and attract a broader audience, thereby increasing subscription revenues over the longer term.

Income Statement for StreamFlix for past and current years:

Last year	£m
Revenue	4,708
Cost of sales	3,808
Gross profit	900
Overheads	767
Operating profit	133
Tax and interest	30
Net profit	103

Current year	£m
Revenue	5,650
Cost of sales	4,232
Gross profit	1,418
Overheads	867
Operating profit	551
Tax and interest	123
Net profit	

Financial planning is critical for StreamFlix as it evaluates the feasibility of bidding for the women's football tournament rights. They anticipate that by having the rights to the tournament, they will also be able to significantly increase their revenue from advertising as well as increasing the number of subscribers. Before committing to such a significant investment, the company's directors recognise the importance of conducting a break-even analysis. By determining the additional number of subscribers needed to cover the increased cost of broadcasting the tournament, StreamFlix can make informed decisions about the potential return on investment and assess the project's financial viability. This strategic approach ensures that StreamFlix remains financially prudent while pursuing growth opportunities that align with its long-term objectives.

Topic 5

EXAMINATION PRACTICE

1. Which **one** of the following is not a finance function? [1]
   A – Advertising price reductions
   B – Anticipating periods of cash flow shortages
   C – Calculating break-even
   D – Managing payments and receipts

2. Which **one** of the following is an internal source of finance? [1]
   A – Hire purchase
   B – Mortgage
   C – Sale of assets
   D – Share issue

3. A business sells products for £12.00. Its fixed costs are £3,200 a month, and the variable cost per unit is £4.50. Calculate the profit if the business sells 600 products a month. [4]

4. Explain **one** way in which a business can improve its cash flow position. [2]

5. Explain **one** benefit to a business of using trade credit. [2]

For the following questions, you must refer to the case study on the previous page.

6. Using the information in the income statement, calculate StreamFlix's net profit margin for the last year. Give your answer to **one** decimal place. [4]

7. StreamFlix expects to make an additional £120m over the next three years from obtaining the rights to the tournament. Using the case study, calculate the ARR if StreamFlix purchases the broadcasting rights. [4]

8. Analyse **one** reason why StreamFlix should calculate the number of extra subscribers it will need to break-even. [3]

9. Analyse StreamFlix's cash position considering its current expansion plans. [3]

10. StreamFlix wants to increase its sports offerings and is considering bidding for the rights to broadcast the next women's international football tournament. It is considering taking out a bank loan to fund this:
    (i) Analyse **one** advantage and **one** disadvantage to StreamFlix of using a bank loan to fund this. [6]
    (ii) Recommend whether StreamFlix should use a bank loan or issue shares to finance the rights. [3]

OCR GCSE **Business**

6.1

ETHICAL AND ENVIRONMENTAL CONSIDERATIONS

As society becomes more aware of ethical and environmental issues, there is growing pressure on businesses to behave responsibly. Although this brings many benefits, it commonly involves a trade-off with profit that may have a negative impact on financial performance.

Ethical considerations and their impact on business

Business ethics involves placing moral values above making profits. This creates a trade-off between profit and being ethically responsible.

- A business may choose to pay workers a fair wage rather than exploiting them.
- A business may choose to improve the working facilities and conditions of employees.
- A business may choose to pay suppliers a fair amount for their materials.
- A business may choose to source resources ethically, e.g. Fairtrade.
- A business may choose to be honest and treat customers fairly.
- A business may choose to avoid making false claims in their marketing.
- A business may choose to be fair to local residents, often investing in community projects to ensure they have a positive impact on society.

Benefits of acting ethically

- Reputational benefits.
- Can be a unique selling point (USP).
- Can be motivating for employees.
- May help to attract more talented workers and it is motivating for existing employees.
- May help to increase sales.
- Suppliers may be more likely to want to work with the business.
- May help to attract more investment.

Drawbacks of acting ethically

- More expensive to source raw materials.
- Training workers to be ethical can be expensive.
- Providing better staff facilities can increase costs.
- Have to charge a higher price, so lose out to lower priced, less ethical businesses.

1. Explain the trade-off between ethical behaviour and profit. [2]

    Behaving ethically, such as paying workers a fair wage for their work, will increase costs.[1] As a result a business will not make as much profit as it possibly could have done.[1]

Environmental considerations and their impact on business

Through its activities, a business has the potential to impact the environment, in the following ways:

Waste disposal

Manufacturing firms are likely to create a lot of waste that needs discarding. Disposing of this waste can be damaging for the environment and local wildlife. Businesses can lessen their impact on the environment by recycling waste and producing products that can be recycled. This limits the amount that is dumped in landfill sites.

Pollution

Some businesses, such as airports, will significantly add to noise pollution in a local area, while a lot of businesses will contribute to poor air quality through either emitting gas in the production process, or simply through an increased amount of traffic on the road.

Climate change

Climate change occurs when average temperatures rise or fall causing weather patterns to change. If a business burns fossil fuels it will add to rising temperatures. Climate change is changing the behaviour of many businesses. 'Greener' businesses may avoid fines for emissions and be able to market themselves as being a more sustainable option, which may increase their market share.

Sustainability

Sustainable production is production that can continue long term and doesn't have a harmful impact on the environment. This can be achieved through:

- Investing in **renewable energy**.
- Using locally sourced materials rather than purchasing from afar, thus reducing their **product miles** and **carbon footprint**.
- Using electric vehicles to distribute products.
- Using biodegradable packaging rather than single-use plastics.
- Recycling or minimising waste.
- Making products from recycled or renewed materials.
- Cleaning up waste and disposing of it properly rather than dumping it.
- Producing products without use of chemicals or other harmful ingredients.

---

2. Identify **two** potential advantages to a business from becoming more environmentally friendly. [2]

The business will gain a better reputation.[1] May attract more customers and therefore increase sales.[1] Other possible answers include: More able to attract investment / Can reduce tax bills / May qualify for grants or subsidies / Can increase price as customers may be willing to pay more / Helps the business become more sustainable.

OCR GCSE **Business**

6.2

THE ECONOMIC CLIMATE

Businesses need to consider changes that are happening in the wider economy. These changes can have a lasting impact on the performance of a business. The level of unemployment will have an effect on the level of consumer spending, which will then ultimately impact the profitability of businesses.

Levels of consumer income

Consumer income (also known as disposable income) is the amount of money that consumers have left to spend after they have paid for all their living expenses and bills.

Economic variables affect the level of **disposable income** through:

- Changes in the level of taxation.
- Changes in the level of unemployment.
- Changes in the interest rate and inflation.
- The economy entering a recession.

Income levels in an economy will have a significant impact on the level of **demand**. If consumers have more disposable income, then the general level of demand for products will increase. This will lead to a business' sales level increasing.

---

1. Explain how an increase in UK average consumer income may impact a business. [2]

    Potential customers will have more money to spend on products.[1] This could lead to an increase in sales for the business.[1]

The answer above is true for a normal or a luxury product. This is a product that will experience an increase in demand when average incomes increase. However, there are products for which this is not always the case, for example, supermarket value products.

Demand for these products actually decreases when average incomes increase as customers switch to buying more branded products.

When faced with a case study, make sure you fully understand what type of product the business is selling and ensure you know how changes in income will affect demand.

Levels of unemployment

Unemployment exists in an economy when there are people of working age who are able to work but cannot find a job.

Rising unemployment

High levels of unemployment can be negative for businesses because:
- More consumers will have less disposable income.
- The level of demand in an economy will fall.
- Sales levels will decrease.
- As demand and sales fall, businesses may need fewer workers, so unemployment rises further.

2. Explain **one** benefit of high unemployment in an economy to a business. [2]

There will be many people who do not have a job,[1] therefore a business will have a greater pool of potential candidates to select from when recruiting.[1]

Alternative answers include: A business may experience lower labour turnover,[1] because there are fewer jobs available for employees to leave for.[1] There will be lots of skilled people out of work,[1] therefore a business can employ people on reduced wage rate.[1]

Falling unemployment

Falling unemployment means that more people are working and there are less people without jobs. This can impact a business in the following ways:
- Potential customers will now have more disposable income.
- May experience an increase in sales as customers spend more.
- It may be more difficult to replace workers who leave.
- The pool of potential applicants for any available position may be smaller than if unemployment was higher.
- They may be unable to recruit enough workers which may impact the ability of the business to function fully.

Given the issues with high and low unemployment, there is a level of 'normal' unemployment at about 4–5% in the developed world which is considered to be acceptable. 0% unemployment is impractical to achieve and can cause considerable societal problems.

OCR GCSE **Business**

6.3

GLOBALISATION

Globalisation is the expansion of trade by businesses to operate across many different countries. It is having an increasing impact on how businesses operate as more compete internationally.

The concept of globalisation

It is much easier for businesses to trade internationally because of the following factors:

Improved technology: The development of e-commerce and telecommunication systems have made it easier for businesses to communicate internationally.

Improvements in global infrastructure and transportation: Better road networks, larger planes and ships have lowered the costs of transporting goods internationally.

Free trade agreements: International trade agreements have removed barriers to trade, such as **tariffs** or **quotas** between countries, encouraging imports and exports.

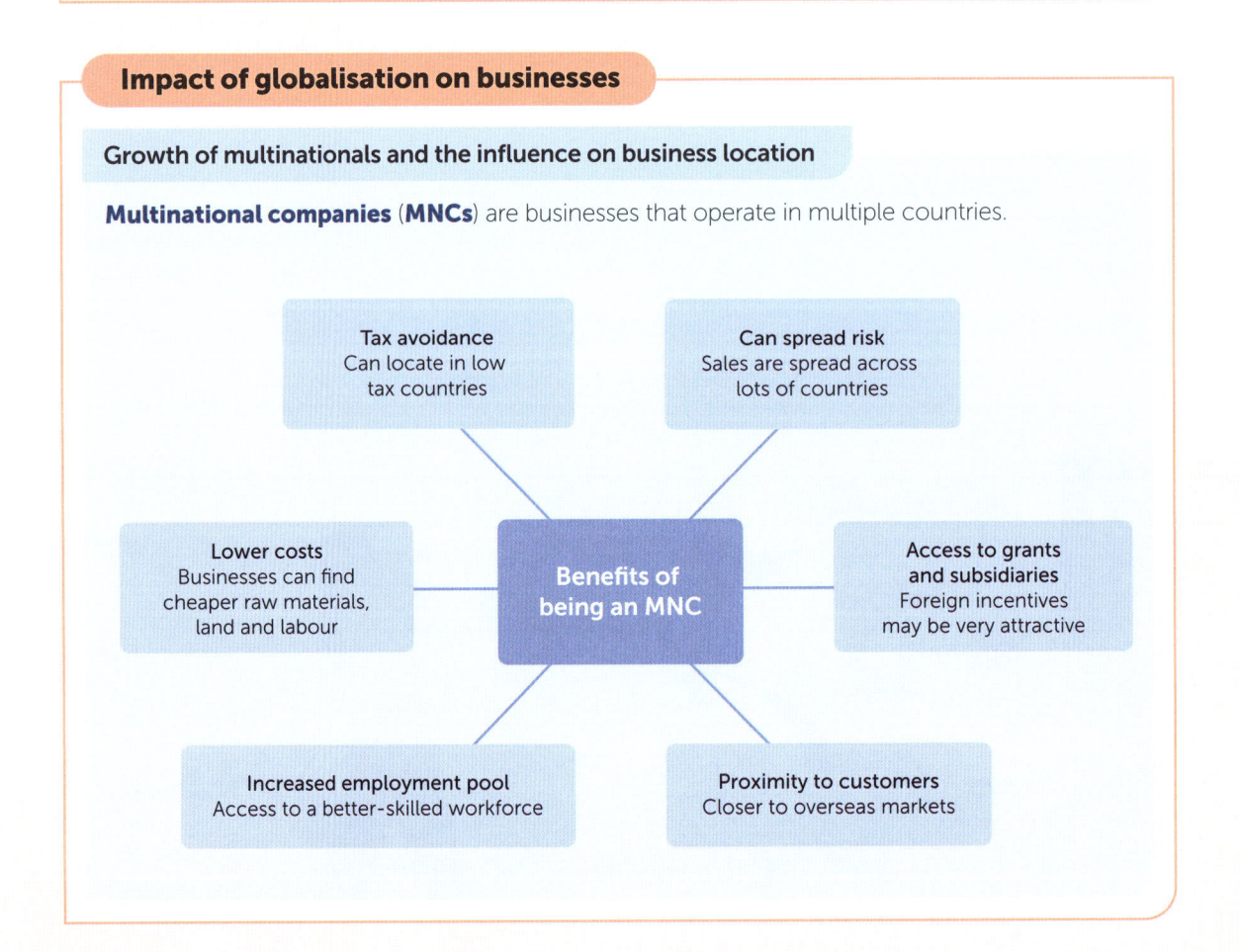

Impact of globalisation on businesses

Growth of multinationals and the influence on business location

Multinational companies (**MNCs**) are businesses that operate in multiple countries.

Benefits of being an MNC

- **Tax avoidance**: Can locate in low tax countries
- **Can spread risk**: Sales are spread across lots of countries
- **Lower costs**: Businesses can find cheaper raw materials, land and labour
- **Access to grants and subsidiaries**: Foreign incentives may be very attractive
- **Increased employment pool**: Access to a better-skilled workforce
- **Proximity to customers**: Closer to overseas markets

Impact of globalisation on businesses continued

How UK businesses compete internationally

Better designs

Product design includes the functionality, appearance and the features of a product. A product that is well designed will help a business to better meet customer needs, therefore they are more likely to purchase the product and improve their loyalty as they become attached to the brand.

Higher quality products at lower prices

A higher quality product is one that better satisfies more customers. When competing internationally, if a business can produce a product that is deemed to be value for money, by being of a higher perceived quality, but priced at a level equal to, or below, products of inferior quality, then a business is more likely to be successful.

International branding

Becoming a multinational will bring with it marketing benefits. A business that operates in many countries will receive more exposure and their products, name and logo will be better known worldwide, increasing brand recognition. However, global brands will have to carefully manage the legal, political, cultural and regulatory requirements and expectations of each country they operate in. Although they will want to maintain brand identity, they will still want to customise their product to appeal to local cultures and preferences, which all costs money!

Benefits and drawbacks of globalisation

Benefits

Rapid growth — Businesses can experience a large increase in sales in a short period of time by selling their products in new overseas markets.

Cheaper resources — Businesses that use materials from abroad in their production process can now potentially get cheaper resources from other overseas suppliers.

Inward investment — Inward investment is when organisations or individuals from overseas invest capital into UK businesses and industries. This has allows businesses to grow, and infrastructure to be improved.

Drawbacks

> Explain **one** drawback to UK business from increased levels of globalisation. [2]
>
> *Increased risk of takeover,[1] because it's now easier for overseas businesses to buy UK companies.[1] / Increased competition in domestic markets,[1] because it's now easier for foreign businesses to start selling their products in the UK.[1]*

OCR GCSE **Business**

Topic 6

CASE STUDY 6

A small, family-owned business, Crunch Delight Ltd has built a name for itself by creating healthy, baked crisps with unique and adventurous flavours. Their product line has offered options including rosemary and beetroot, truffle and sea salt, and even a tangy pineapple and chilli blend. These unusual flavour combinations became the brand's unique selling point (USP), attracting health-conscious consumers and adventurous foodies alike. Over the years, Crunch Delight grew into a stronger brand in the UK, expanding its presence in supermarkets and organic food stores.

However, as demand increased, the company's operating costs in the UK soared. In a controversial move, Crunch Delight decided to shut down its UK operations and shift its manufacturing to Estonia in Eastern Europe, where wages were considerably lower, and production was more cost-effective. The company framed the decision as a necessary step to keep their products affordable and competitive, especially as the market for premium snacks became more saturated. The management claimed that moving to Eastern Europe would allow them to maintain their commitment to health-conscious consumers without compromising the quality of their crisps.

Despite the company's justification, the UK press was quick to criticise the decision, accusing Crunch Delight of prioritising profit over people. Several media outlets published stories condemning the move, stating that it had displaced hundreds of workers and harmed the local economy in areas where the factories once operated. This backlash hurt Crunch Delight's image in the UK, with many loyal customers questioning the brand's values and whether it still stood for the ethical principles it once promoted.

In response to the criticism, Crunch Delight defended their decision to move to Estonia, stating that it wasn't just about cutting costs but also about making the business more sustainable. Estonia's access to renewable energy sources, such as wind and solar power, allowed the company to reduce its carbon footprint and power its new factory with cleaner energy. The company emphasised that sustainability was a core part of their mission, and the move aligned with their long-term goal of reducing environmental impact. Additionally, the high unemployment rate in Estonia provided an opportunity for recruitment, allowing the company to find skilled workers more easily and contribute to the local economy.

Furthermore, relocating to Estonia opened up new avenues for growth within the European market. With excellent transportation links, Crunch Delight could distribute their products across Europe more efficiently, positioning themselves to sell in a wider range of countries. As part of their expansion plan, the company announced that they would tailor the flavours of their crisps to suit the preferences of the local populations, adapting their signature adventurous combinations to reflect regional tastes. However, Crunch Delight acknowledged that this would come with challenges, particularly in navigating the varying laws and regulations on food preparation and labelling across different countries. Despite these issues, they saw this as an exciting opportunity to broaden their appeal and introduce their unique brand of healthy crisps to a larger, more diverse audience.

Topic 6

EXAMINATION PRACTICE

1. Which **one** of the following is an example of ethical treatment of a workforce? [1]
   A – Allow flexible working
   B – Cut wages in order to save money
   C – Replace employees with robots
   D – Reduce the number of breaks for employees

2. A country is experiencing rising incomes among their population.
   Which of the following actions is most likely, where a business is selling a unique product? [1]
   A – Cut employees
   B – Increase price
   C – Offer discounts
   D – Reduce costs

3. Identify **two** reasons why a multinational might choose to locate in another country. [2]

4. Explain **one** factor that has led to increased globalisation. [2]

5. Explain **one** way a business can behave ethically towards its customers. [2]

6. Explain **one** reason why a business should behave ethically. [2]

For the following questions, you must refer to the case study on the previous page.

7. Explain **one** positive and **one** negative impact on the environment from Crunch Delight's decision to relocate to Eastern Europe. [4]

8. Analyse **one** benefit to Crunch Delight from the high levels of unemployment in Estonia. [3]

9. (a) Analyse **one** benefit to Crunch Delight arising from its decision to sell in multiple European countries. [3]
   (b) Analyse **one** drawback to Crunch Delight arising from its decision to sell in multiple European countries. [3]
   (c) Recommend whether it is the right decision for Crunch Delight to sell in multiple European countries. [3]

OCR GCSE **Business**

THE INTERDEPENDENT NATURE OF BUSINESS

This section is different to sections 1–6. It does not look at new theory, but instead refers to the links between different areas of business across both exam papers that affect decision making, the risks and rewards of business activity and the use of financial information in measuring and understanding business performance and decision making.

The interdependent nature of business operations

The interdependencies of business functions, such as finance, marketing, operations, and human resources, are crucial for decision-making. Each area relies on others for information and resources.

How these interdependencies underpin business decision making

To understand how the different functional areas impact on each other, consider the following scenario:

A manufacturing business has decided to expand. One strategy they used to achieve this goal is to heavily advertise their product. The promotional campaign proved to be successful and now the decision of the marketing department has impacted the other functional areas.

Finance – The advertising campaign would require a substantial budget. The finance to cover this has to be obtained from an appropriate source. The finance department may need to set increased budgets for the operations department as they may need to increase their productive capacity. They will also need to finance any extra staff that may be required.

Operations – The operations department may need to increase their production. This would mean liaising with suppliers to see if they can supply the increased volume of raw materials. Logistics would be impacted as they would have to deliver to more locations.

Human resources – The HR department would need to recruit new workers which would be time consuming. Once they have appointed new workers, they would need to train them, which can also be costly and time consuming.

Impact of risk and reward on business activity

When making decisions, businesses need to consider the impact that potential risks could have on the performance of the business. Risks and rewards are discussed in more detail in **Section 1.1** earlier in this book, however businesses must consider:

- The potential that new rivals could enter the market and affect sales levels, prices that a business can charge and ultimately revenue and profit levels.
- There could be changes in costs, including an increase in wages and materials. Decisions on changes in wage levels will be impacted by both internal and external factors, such as the economic climate. Material costs could be impacted by world shortages, exchange rate changes or problems with transportation.

Use of financial information in measuring and understanding business performance and decision making

Businesses use financial information to help make decisions. This information can be either past records, such as financial accounts from previous years, or it could be financial predictions for the future such as cash flow forecasts.

> Explain **one** drawback to a business from using financial records to make decisions about future business activity. [2]
>
> *Financial records present historical data and there is no guarantee that what happened previously will happen again.[1] Therefore, a business may make decisions on production levels assuming sales will continue at their current level which may not be the case.[1]*

The final question on Paper 2 will be a 9 mark evaluation question about the interdependent nature of business. This includes a question about:

- How an aspect of a business' activity (e.g. their customer service) could impact on the business' performance.
- How financial information could impact on a business' decision making about its future activities.
- How an aspect of a business' activity (e.g. its manufacturing process) could impact the risks and rewards a business faces.

Topic 7

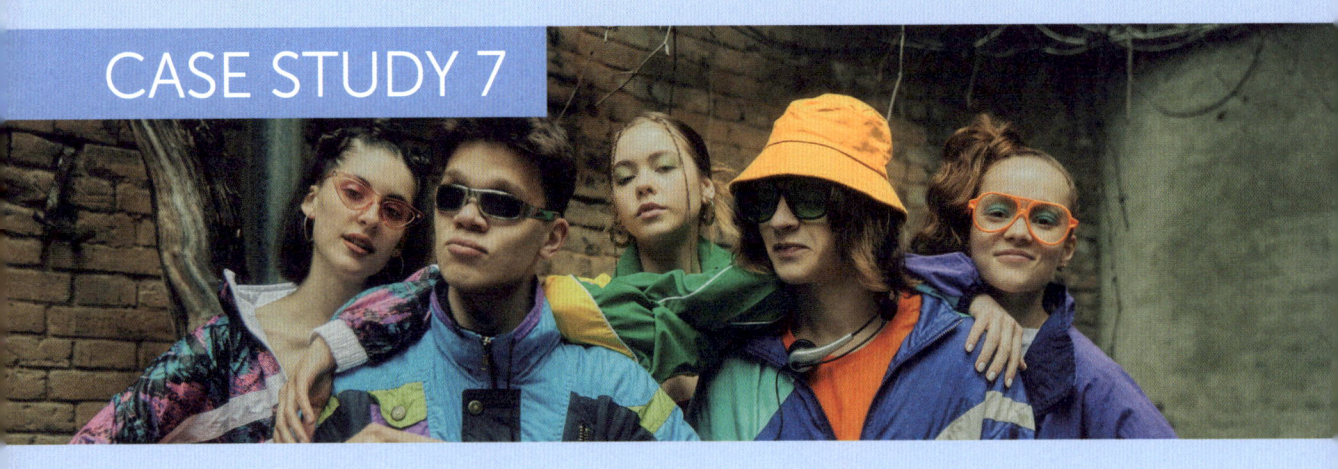

CASE STUDY 7

Over the past five years Urban Trend Ltd, a well-established clothing retailer, has experienced steady and continuous growth in both sales and profits, as evidenced by its financial accounts. The company's ability to maintain strong customer loyalty, combined with an expanding product range, has helped drive consistent revenue increases year on year. Strategic investments in physical store upgrades and a well-integrated online platform have contributed to this growth, allowing the retailer to offer a seamless shopping experience both in-store and online.

However, the retail landscape is shifting dramatically with the rise of new, online-only competitors. These emerging brands are leveraging aggressive social media marketing tactics, targeting younger consumers with highly engaging and interactive content. Platforms like Instagram and TikTok have become powerful tools for these new entrants, enabling them to quickly build brand awareness and reach a large audience without the overheads of maintaining physical stores. As a result, they are attracting a significant portion of the market, especially among tech-savvy and trend-conscious shoppers.

Despite its solid financial performance, Urban Trend faces increasing pressure from these online newcomers. While its traditional marketing strategies and loyal customer base have served it well, the company may need to adapt its approach to stay competitive. A stronger focus on digital engagement and innovative social media campaigns could be necessary to capture the attention of younger consumers and maintain its market position in an evolving retail environment.

Topic 7

EXAMINATION PRACTICE

1. The Marketing Director of a manufacturer of traditional British microwaveable meals has suggested that they extend its range to incorporate a new range of microwaveable pasta and Asian dishes. They have presented their suggestion to the board of directors.

   Which **one** of the following is not likely to encourage the board of directors to agree to the extension of the range? [1]

   A – The opportunity to gain a reputation in providing a choice for consumers

   B – The opportunity to gain greater discounts from suppliers through bulk buying

   C – The opportunity to gain more customers than rivals

   D – The opportunity to increase the financial risks of the business

2. A cleaning business is looking to use spare staff capacity to offer services to a wider pool of customers.

   As a result of this action, which **one** of the following actions is of most importance? [1]

   A – The finance function will have to spend time training new employees

   B – The HR function will have to recruit and interview potential employees

   C – The purchasing function will need to find cheaper suppliers of raw materials

   D – The marketing function will need to start generating awareness

3. Explain **one** way in which the operations department can have an impact on the marketing function. [2]

4. Explain **one** way in which the HR department could have an impact on the finance function. [2]

For the following question, you must refer to the case study on the previous page.

5. Evaluate how using financial information may impact on the future performance of Urban Trend. [9]

OCR GCSE **Business**

EXAMINATION PRACTICE ANSWERS

Mark allocations are indicated by the use of [1].
[K] indicates where a mark is gained for demonstrating **knowledge** (AO1a)
[U] indicates where **understanding** has been demonstrated. (AO1b)
[APP] indicates where a mark is gain for **application** of knowledge. (AO2)
[AN] indicates where a mark is gained through **analysis**, covering Assessment Objective 3a (AO3a)
[EVAL] indicates where a mark is gained through the use of **evaluation**. (AO3b).

Section 1

1. B. Profit. [1]

2. A. Can raise large amounts of finance through selling shares to the public. [1]

3. Spotting a business opportunity.[1] Developing an idea for a business.[1] Satisfying the needs of consumers.[1] [2]

4. Profits need to be shared amongst the partners.[1] Therefore the owners may receive less income than if they set it up alone.[1] Partners face unlimited liability,[1] which means they are personally responsible for the debts of the business.[1] Partners may not agree on key decisions,[1] which may damage relationships / cause unnecessary delay / detract from the focus of the business.[1] [2]

5. Businesses may be at different stages of development.[1] One business may be starting out and will need to focus on survival, while an established business may be looking to grow.[1] Different business may face different wider market / economic issues, [1] which may benefit some businesses and threaten others.[1] Different products may suit different markets / issues, [1] which may benefit some while threatening the success of others.[1] Owners may have different motivations for running the business, [1] so some may want to maximise profit while others wish to benefit those in the community ahead of any profits.[1] [2]

6. A business' supplier may decide to increase their prices for their products.[1] Therefore the business' costs may increase.[1] A supplier may cease trading / no longer be able to get that material / part,[1] causing a business customer to seek an alternative supplier which may change the design / taste / function of a product.[1] [2]

7. Richard showed that he was a risk-taker.[1] This is because he invested his savings in the fitness centres.[APP] Creativity / determination[1] because he had a clear idea / vision and planned meticulously to make things succeed.[1] Confidence[1] in his own ideas to invest his own money.[1] [2]

8. One risk that they both face is financial loss.[1] This is because Richard invested his savings and Vikram also contributed financially, so these investments could be lost if the fitness centres fail.[APP] Reputational damage[1] may be done if the centres fail as Richard's name is associated with the enterprise.[APP] [2]

9. One benefit is that the owners will have limited liability.[1] This means that Richard and Vikram are seen as separate to the business, so can only lose the amount of their savings that they invested should fitness centres fail.[APP] This means that they face less risk as their personal possessions will not be at risk.[AN] The business will be able to sell shares privately.[1] This would raise further finance for growth [AN] should they need it to acquire another gym. [APP] [3]

10. One reason was so that he could help to convince people to invest in the fitness centres, helping the venture to succeed.[1] This allowed him to obtain a bank loan from the bank.[APP] Therefore Richard had enough cash to set up his first fitness centre.[AN] Thorough planning helps to reduce risk. [1] It considers issues in the future with different strategies for growth with each new gym,[APP] and enabled him to foresee issues before they became a problem.[AN] [3]

11. One reward is self-satisfaction.[1] This is because Richard is a fitness enthusiast and wants to ensure people have an affordable way to stay fit and healthy.[APP] Therefore in having more people use his fitness centres he will have a sense of achievement.[AN] Richard and Vikram may seek financial reward. [1] This is because they will want to earn something back on their initial investments [APP] that is above what they could get with less-risky options. [AN] [3]

12. Customers / local community will be most affected,[1] this is because more customers will have more opportunity to attend fitness classes / there will be more fitness centres in new locations nationwide.[1] [2]

13. Horizontal integration is when Stabler Gyms would merge or takeover another fitness centre.[K] Acquiring a competitor gym would allow Stabler Gyms to increase its market share from the 5% it currently has,[APP] which would increase the number of members that it has already.[U] Thus, allowing the fitness centres to become established nationwide rather than just in the region that they currently operate in.[APP] This would increase revenue from the increased membership.[AN] However, taking over another fitness centre may not be beneficial for Stabler Gyms because there is a lot of risk involved.[U] This is because Richard has identified that there may be cultural clashes and integration issues. [APP] This may mean that they lose their reputation for being an affordable option for people to stay fit and healthy.[AN] I think they should grow through horizontal integration.[EVAL] Richard and Vikram's business does not have a presence outside their region and merging with, or taking over a fitness club that has centres in other areas is the quickest way that they can increase their market share nationally.[EVAL] This does depend on how much they will have to pay to take over their rival, but as long as it is a reasonable price then it will be worth it.[EVAL] [9]

Section 2

1. B. 20%. [1]
2. C. The opinions of the local population on hairstyles. [1]
3. Two from: Introduction,[1] Growth,[1] Maturity,[1] Decline.[1] [2]
4. To spread risk.[1] This is because should sales of one product start to fall, a business could still be receiving large revenues from sales of its other products.[1] To enable higher growth. [1] This is because different products will appeal to other market segments enabling greater sales.[1] Increased turnover.[1] This is because customers are more likely to buy product bundles of several products in the same purchase increasing the average sale value.[1] [2]
5. Higher volume of sales as the price is set low.[1] This will lead to a larger market share for the business than if they charged a high price.[1] Low initial prices help to limit competition[1] because newer entrants to the market will find it harder to match the lower prices.[1] Increases uptake among customers / brand loyalty[1] as the initial price is more affordable / less of a barrier to adopting the brand.[1] [2]
6. If a business decides to produce a high quality product they will likely have to set a high price,[1] because it will cost the business more to produce.[1] A premium product[1] is more likely to command a high price in order to maintain exclusivity.[1] A product with few unique features over the competition[1] may need to compete on price over anything else so a lower price will need to be offered.[1] [2]
7. One reason is to find out customers opinions in depth,[1] which helped the owners of Porkey's to discover whether there would be a enough demand for their cured meats.[APP] / Porkey's already had direct contact with their target market[1] through their direct-to-consumer sales at farmers' markets.[APP] [2]
8. Porkey's could segment the market by income.[1] This is because they discovered through census data that the population of the local area had a higher than average level of income.[APP] / Porkey's could segment the market by those who value animal welfare / ethically sourced meats[1] as they only use meat from free-range livestock.[APP] [2]
9. Porkey's uses retailers to reach a larger number of customers.[1] This is because they sell their cured meats through nationwide supermarket chains.[APP] As a result they will sell more packs of chorizo and salami.[AN] / Retailers can increase sales of stock outside of Porkey's local area and farmers' markets[1] as they have nationwide chains[APP] This increases their market reach with outlets over a much wider geographical area.[AN] [3]
10. One reason is so that potential customers might feel inclined to buy the product after trying it.[1] This is because when they try it they will realise how nice the meat tastes.[APP] As a result Porkey's will see an increase in sales as shown by the fact that 73% who taste the meat make a purchase.[AN] / Free samples generate brand loyalty as customers like getting something for nothing.[1] They can also experience the quality of the product without the barrier to purchase[APP] which increases brand familiarity / creates a positive brand association / enables them to start a conversation to gather feedback.[AN] [3]
11. Porkey's can find out information on the local population.[1] For example, through researching census data, Porkey's found out that the local population have a higher than average level of income.[APP] This would allow Porkey's to use a price skimming strategy when selling their meats.[AN] / Secondary research is usually quicker and easier to gather.[1] Census data has already been collected and made available[APP] which means that decisions can be made in less time / more efficiently / at less cost, keeping overall costs down.[1] [3]
12. Porkey's should use their own website to advertise the charcuterie boards.[EVAL] This is because customers will be able to see the all the meats, cheeses and local produce on the board which they couldn't do on the radio.[EVAL] Therefore the food will look more appealing and there will be more chance that a sale will be made.[EVAL]

    Porkey's should use the radio to advertise their boards[EVAL] as this will reach a greater audience who aren't already aware of the website address.[EVAL] Therefore, they will increase their brand awareness and increase sales from new customers.[EVAL] [3]
13. Porkey's should introduce the new line of charcuterie boards because they have identified demand for the meats and local produce.[K] This is because the market data they have collected suggests that there is a growing trend of people opting to host dinner parties at home rather than eating out,[APP] which would mean that their sales levels would grow.[U] This would increase the revenue of the cured meat company.[AN] However, producing and delivering the new boards may be expensive.[U] This is because there will be a lot of ingredients to put onto the boards such as the cured meats and other ingredients.[APP] This will mean that the business will have to charge a higher price for the boards.[AN] I think that they should introduce the new charcuterie boards.[EVAL] The business has grown by 42% over the last two years, demonstrating that there is demand for their meats.[EVAL] However, this does depend on whether the customers will be willing to pay the higher price to have the boards delivered. If it is too high, they may just choose to eat out instead.[EVAL] [9]

OCR GCSE **Business – Answers**

Section 3

1. A. It may take longer for shoppers to get their groceries scanned through the till. [1]
2. C. The employee's salary and benefits. [1]
3. Two from: Pay,[1] bonus,[1] profit share,[1] fringe benefits.[1] [2]
4. To detail the skills and characteristics that are required,[1] therefore helping to ensure that only suitable candidates apply, saving the business time.[1] A person specification helps a business to fairly assess the suitability of candidates on their abilities related to the role[1] which helps to avoid bias / prejudice / discrimination which can cause problems in recruiting successfully.[1] [2]
5. Staff will be happier in their work,[1] therefore they are more likely to provide a better level of customer service / quality of output.[1] Motivated staff are less likely to be late / absent / leave[1] improving punctuality / productivity / staff retention.[1] [2]
6. Internal promotion can be motivating for employees,[1] therefore they may work harder in order to show management that they are capable and deserving of a job higher up the hierarchy.[1] The employee will already know the business / and the business them,[1] so less induction training is needed / less chance of their being a clash with company culture or personalities. Faster, easier and cheaper way to recruit,[1] which saves the business time and costs.[1] [2]
7. Training on how to log in to the design software.[1] Training on the process of providing customers with sample designs.[1] Training on how to use the digital communication tools.[1] Training on the systems and processes in order to maintain the high standards / reputation of the business.[1] [2]
8. It is important so that they can clearly communicate with customers,[1] because their clients are based all over the globe and they will use video conferencing to show their clients their initial designs[APP]. RDS employees can all communicate with each other remotely[1] as they can be employed on a flexible working from home basis.[APP] [2]
9. Having a flat structure allows more delegation to take place,[1] therefore graphic designers will have more authority when making decisions on the type of designs they produce for their clients.[APP] Flat structures have a shorter chain of command[1] which improves communication.[1] [2]
10. One benefit is that home-working can be more attractive / motivating,[1] therefore it is more likely to attract more designers to come and work for Francisco,[APP] enabling the business to maintain its reputation for high quality graphic designs.[AN] Remote working means that Francisco can recruit from a much wider field / globally[1] which will help him to find the top-tier designers he needs[APP] as he has a far greater number of potential people that he could recruit to choose from.[AN] RDS can avoid having to provide office space for remote employees[1] as they can connect to others using the communication software tools.[APP] This saves on office costs.[AN] [3]
11. (a) (i) Interviews allow one to one conversations to occur,[1] therefore managers will be able to carefully ask questions to assess a candidate's knowledge of design software and their experiences in graphic design.[APP] As a result, it will help Francisco to employ the most suitable designer for the role.[AN] Interviews happen face-to-face[1] which helps managers to introduce them to the rest of the creative or sales team[APP] to assess cultural fit and personality.[AN] [3]
    (ii) Ravenelli can set a task where candidates have to work together,[1] for instance Francisco could give them a design brief in which they have a certain amount of time to collaborate and come up with a website design,[APP] this will then allow the business to see which of the designers have good communication skills and can work well as part of a team.[AN] Group activities allow people to show leadership skills and understanding.[1] This means that Francisco can assess professional characteristics as well as design skills[APP] to ensure that they fit well into the right role within the sales or creative teams.[AN] [3]
    (b) Interviews are the best way to select designers,[EVAL] because Francisco and the managers will really know if they understand graphic design which group activities may not highlight,[EVAL] as they can ask specific questions about software and the design process.[EVAL]
    Group activities are best to assess practical skills[EVAL] as they provide an insight into how a person approaches a task and their level of skill[EVAL] which improves the chance of recruiting the right person into the team.[EVAL] [3]
12. Apprenticeships are government backed schemes where the employee will conduct a mixture of learning on-the-job and off-the-job training.[K] Therefore, apprentice designers will be able to learn theory in college but also get hands on experience of the bespoke design software from people who are already using it,[APP] The business can ensure that the training is tailored to the apprentice[U] so they can develop their designing skills in a way that suits the business.[AN] However, by offering apprenticeships, the business is employing a less experienced designer,[U] because they will have had no experience in using the bespoke design software and therefore may not be able to produce as high quality designs as someone who has been a graphic designer for a number of years.[APP] As a result, Ravenelli Design Solutions may damage their reputation for producing high standard designs.[AN] I think that it will be beneficial for Ravenelli Design Solutions to continue to offer apprenticeships.[EVAL] Francisco has always invested in people and sees it as key to his business' success, so by giving new designers a start in the industry and using the most experienced designers to train them up will keep them loyal to the business.[EVAL] It also means that RDS can mould them into their way of working[AN] and generate opportunities to recruit internally by making them a permanent employee once their apprenticeship period has finished.[K] This does depend on ensuring that they are capable of producing high quality designs before letting them work on their own with clients, so the brand's reputation is not ruined.[EVAL] [9]

Section 4

1. D - Supply a phone of satisfactory quality. [1]

2. C - Productivity is likely to increase. [1]

3. Defective products will not make it to market.[1] This is because technology / an inspector is employed to check the quality of products at the end of the production line so faulty products will be removed.[1] The business may gain a positive reputation[1] as people notice / report on social media the consistent quality of their products / satisfaction with their purchases.[1] [2]

4. It will be more convenient for customers to travel to / customers may prefer to purchase goods from local suppliers.[1] Therefore they are much more likely to purchase from the business, increasing sales.[1] The business may sell perishable goods / goods that are difficult to transport or send by delivery[1] so being close to their market means they save on costs / customers can collect larger products directly.[1] [2]

5. The business will be able to gain supplies at the best possible price[1] therefore they can lower the price charged to customers, increasing sales.[1] Supplies will be trusted to be delivered on time / as ordered[1] which reduces any problems with production and associated costs / prevents delays in getting goods to the customer, affecting customer service / reputation.[1] Waste is reduced[1] which can lower costs / improve output / production times.[1] [2]

6. An e-commerce system makes it easier for people to place orders.[1] This is because confectionery retailers that may not have previously stocked their sweets, may now be more likely to purchase from them with an easier ordering system / at times outside of the normal retail hours.[APP] As a result the confectionery business may experience an increase in sales which could potentially lead to greater profit.[AN] [3]

7. Sweet Delights could provide excellent knowledge of / product information on the sweets.[1] This is because SweetDelights Ltd sells to retailers / wholesalers who then sell the sweets onto the end consumer.[1] As a result, a retailer will need to know about the ingredients used in the sweets and information about their nutritional value / allergies,[APP] as they will need to pass this information onto the person that consumes the sweets.[AN] [3]

8. Flow production allows SweetDelights to mass produce their sweets.[1] As they are manufacturing such large quantities of the confectionery, they can buy the ingredients (such as SugarX) in large quantities.[1] As a result, the supplier is more likely to offer a discount for buying the sugar in bulk / large quantities over time.[APP]

   Flow production likely means that the average cost of producing a bag of sweets is reduced. [1] This will allow the business to sell the sweets to retailers for a lower price / increase the profit per bag,[APP] resulting in the manufacturer becoming more competitive against other confectionery firms / increasing overall profits.[1]

   The confectionery company has been able to introduce technology to the production process.[1] This allows the sweets to be made identically each time. [APP]

   The machinery / robotics necessary for mass production involve a very high initial cost.[1] These will then need regular servicing and maintenance by skilled engineers.[APP] / Production line maintenance staff may need to be additionally employed,[1] increasing the overhead costs.[APP]

   Sweet Delights may benefit from reduced payroll as the production line may replace a lot of manual labour roles. [1] Those remaining on the production line may become more specialist[1] at their individual jobs which would boost productivity.[APP] Staff working on a flow production line may suffer from fatigue / find the repetition will demotivate them,[1] lowering productivity.[APP] [6]

9. It is important as the confectionery firm has built up a reputation for manufacturing high quality sweets.[1] Therefore, the end consumers will expect the sweets to continue to be of a consistently high quality all the time in future.[APP] This will be a source of differentiation for the sweet manufacturer and therefore means that they can charge a higher price for a bag of sweets.[AN] [3]

10. The advantage of switching to Supplier B is that it is offering SugarX at a lower price.[K] Therefore, the cost of ingredients may be lower, and variable costs are reduced.[U] As a result, the average cost of producing each bag of sweets will be lower.[APP] This will allow SweetDelights to lower the price to its customers / the retail outlets where the bags of sweets are sold.[APP] The hope is that this would result in sales increasing[AN] which would increase the revenue[K] and therefore potentially the profit of the confectionery firm.[AN]

    In conclusion I believe that they should stick with their existing supplier rather than changing to Supplier B.[EVAL] This is because the confectionery firm has worked hard to build up its reputation and reliable delivery is a crucial part of that process.[EVAL] However, my decision depends on whether their current supplier can continue to deliver SugarX at reasonable prices. If they become too expensive then Supplier B may just be worth the risk.[EVAL] [9]

OCR GCSE **Business – Answers**

Section 5

1. A - Advertising price reductions. [1]

2. C - Sale of assets. [1]

3. Revenue = 600 × £12 = 7,200;[1] Total variable costs = 600 × 4.50 = £2,700;[1] Total cost = 3,200 + 2,700 = 5,900;[1] Profit = 7,200 − 5,900 = £1,300[1] [4]

4. A business can improve its cash flow is by agreeing an overdraft with the bank.[1] This will allow the business to be able to continue to withdraw money from their bank account even when it has a negative balance, so they can make any necessary payments.[1]

   A business could apply for a loan.[1] This should increase the available cash amount to be able to pay for any additional costs / cover the expected period of shortfall in income.[1]

   Unused assets could be sold[1] in order to raise sufficient finance to cover any period of shortfall.[1]

   Agreements with trade suppliers could be renegotiated to increase the period of trade credit.[1] This would provide an extended period where cash outflows are reduced.[1]

   A business owner could support the business with an injection of cash from their own funds / raised from friends and family.[1] This would provide a positive boost to cash flow which could help a business to get through a period where income was less than expected / outgoings were more than expected.[1] [2]

5. One benefit of using trade credit is that a business can purchase supplies without having to pay for them immediately. [1] This can enable the business to sell the products to the customers and receive payment from them before they need to pay the supplier.[1] [2]

6. Net profit for current year = 551m − 123m[1] = £428m[1] Net profit margin = (428 ÷ 5650) × 100[1] = 7.6%[1] [4]

7. Average rate of return = (Average return per annum ÷ Initial investment) × 100. Answer = 8% [4]
   Average return per annum = 120 ÷ 3[1] = £40m;[1] Average rate of return = (40 ÷ 500) × 100[1] = 8%[1] [4]

8. StreamFlix should calculate the number of extra subscribers needed to break even because it will show the streaming company whether investing in the women's football tournament is viable[1]. This is because it will show whether the extra number needed to cover the £500m investment is realistic[APP]. If it didn't conduct this financial analysis, then the media company may end up in financial difficulty because they would invest significant funds into the bid[AN]. [3]

9. Cash is the money that StreamFlix has in its bank account to spend.[1] It currently is in a strong position with a large positive bank balance,[APP] so the bank may be prepared to lend money to them as they have good liquidity.[AN] [6]

10. (i) The advantage of using a bank loan to pay for the purchase of the rights to the women's football tournament is that no control is lost when this method is used because the existing shareholders retain their same percentage ownership and current directors will remain in control.[1] This means that they can continue on their current strategy of promoting sports to a diverse range of customers,[APP] which means that the philosophy of the business continues which has proven successful, as last year's net profit of £428 proves.[AN]

    However, using a bank loan will require the television entertainment company to pay the loan back with interest.[1] This can hugely increase the fixed costs, which is particularly true for the streaming firm as they are looking to borrow up to £500m.[APP] This will lead to increased total costs, which therefore may lead to the television streaming company having to increase the price of their subscriptions.[AN] [6]

    (ii) I recommend that StreamFlix use a bank loan.[EVAL] This is because they are in a strong liquid position as they have a large positive bank balance.[EVAL] Issuing shares would dilute the current ownership and mean that they may move away from their position of broadcasting a diverse range of sports to only concentrating on a few.[EVAL] [3]

Section 6

1. A. Allow flexible working. [1]

2. B. Increase price. [1]

3. Two from: Lower level of taxation, [1] Lower costs of production, [1] Availability of skilled labour, [1] Proximity to customers, [1] Proximity to raw materials. [1] [2]

4. Improved technology.[1] The emergence or development of e-commerce has allowed businesses to more easily sell abroad / more people are connected to Internet devices that enable online shopping. [1]

   Improvements in global infrastructure and transportation [1] have resulted in better road networks / larger planes / ships which have lowered the costs of transporting / delivering goods / raw materials internationally.[1]

   Free trade agreements [1] have removed barriers to trade / tariffs or quotas between countries / encourage imports and exports. [1] [2]

5. A business should be honest in its marketing of its products.[1] This means that consumers will not be misled by the business.[1] A business may do more for the community [1] where its customers are more likely to be based / feel an impact. [1] Strong after-sales support may be offered (for product queries / returns / repairs) [1] so customers don't feel ignored and uncared for. [1] Products may be developed / tested so that they are safe for use [1] and pass all necessary standards. [1] [2]

6. Behaving ethically means that the business could receive a positive reputation. [1] This could lead to more ethically conscious customers purchasing products from the business over its competitors. [1] Working for an ethical business can be motivating for employees [1] who feel that there is a greater purpose / force for good in what the company is trying to achieve. [1] An ethical company may attract more talented workers / better suppliers / investors [1] who would rather be associated with them over a less ethical company. [1] [2]

7. One positive impact is that the business will utilise more renewable energy rather than fossil fuels. [1] As a result the crisp manufacturer will not be contributing as much to global warming. [APP]
One negative impact is that the product will have to be transported large distances to reach markets. [1] Crisps for the UK market will have to be transported back to the UK, causing a larger carbon footprint. [APP] [4]

8. One benefit is that there will be a large pool of potential workers to select from. [1] The crisp manufacturer would require a large number of people to work in their factory having relocated from the UK. [APP] This means that they won't need to spend as much cash in the recruitment process. [AN]

Crunch Delight may experience lower labour turnover,[1] because there are fewer jobs available in Estonia for employees to leave for. [APP] This means that the company will save money on retention and ongoing recruitment costs. [AN] There will be lots of skilled people out of work,[1] so the competition for jobs in Estonia will be higher,[APP] therefore a business can employ people on reduced wage rate. [AN] [3]

9. (a) One benefit is that sales may increase. [1] This is because there will be a lot of people who will like the fact that the manufacturer tailors the crisps to the tastes of the local markets, [APP] which means that they are more likely to purchase the crisps and Crunch Delight will see increased revenues and profits. [AN]
Sales may increase. [1] This is because the overall market size across Europe is much larger, [APP] which means that they have more potential customers. [AN]
Company risk is spread over more countries [1] because sales in each country may peak and trough at different rates, [APP] which means that the most successful countries will support others where sales are lower. [AN] [3]

(b) There may be increased costs of manufacturing.[1] This is because each country will have different health and safety rules with regards to food and labelling of food, so the business will have to produce different labels for each country. [APP] As a result, variable costs may increase, causing profit margins to reduce. [AN] [3]

(c) The increased cost of manufacturing in changing the crisps to suit the tastes of local markets and to produce the labels that meet that country's legal requirements is likely to be more than offset by the increase in sales. [EVAL] I therefore think that selling to a wider customer base will have the greater impact. [EVAL] This is especially true because the business can sell its crisps for a higher price as they are seen as unique. [EVAL] [3]

Section 7

1. D. The opportunity to increase the financial risks of the business. [1]
2. D. The marketing function will need to start generating awareness. [1]
3. The operations department, through research and development, may come up with new unique features for its product / open a new store in a different location / introduce ecommerce functionality. [1] This would mean the marketing function would need to promote this so that customers are made aware. [1] [2]
4. If the HR department decide that they want to introduce new company wide team building training days to improve morale, [1] it would cost money, and the finance function would need to budget for them. [1] [2]
5. Financial information includes financial statements and forecasts. [K] These can be used to help judge the future performance of a business. [U] One benefit to the clothing retailer of using financial information is that it can offer an insight into trends and patterns in sales, for example that Urban Trend has seen a steady increase in revenue and profits over the past 5 years. [APP] This may indicate they could expect a similar sales pattern in the future, suggesting that the business will continue to be successful. [AN]

One drawback in using financial statements is that they are no guarantee that any trends will continue for Urban Trend, particularly as many online-only retailers have changed the market with aggressive social media marketing campaigns. [APP] This may mean sales don't continue to rise, and the fashion retailer faces a fight to keep a hold of its current customers. [AN]

Financial information can have a positive impact in making future decisions, [EVAL] although its use will be limited, and it should not be used in isolation when making decisions. [EVAL] This is because there are other non-financial factors and risks, such as the emergence of the online only retailers that aren't accounted for in the financial statements but will have an impact on Urban Trend's success. [EVAL] [9]

FORMULAE

Revenue	Selling price × Number of units sold
Total variable costs	Variable cost per unit × Number of units sold
Total costs	Fixed costs + Variable costs
Profit	Revenue − Total costs
Cost per unit	Total costs ÷ Number of units sold
Margin of safety	Actual output − Break even output
Net cash flow	Total receipts − Total payments
Closing balance	Opening balance + Net cash flow
Total assets	Non-current assets + Current assets
Net assets	(Non-current assets + Current assets) − (Current liabilities + Non-current liabilities)
Gross profit	Revenue − Cost of sales
Operating profit	Gross profit − Overheads
Net profit	Operating profit − Tax and interest
Gross profit margin	(Gross profit ÷ Revenue) × 100
Net profit margin	(Net profit ÷ Revenue) × 100
ARR	(Average annual profit ÷ cost of investment) × 100
Percentage change	(Change in figures ÷ Original figure) × 100
Average	Total of all the individual values ÷ The number of values in the set

> ⭐ You may have to demonstrate your basic quantitative skills as well as potentially being asked to use business calculations. This could include calculating the percentage change between two figures or calculating the average of a set of data.
>
> You will not be provided with formulae in the exam.

INDEX

Symbols
4Ps 25, 32

A
academic development 50
added value 60
advertising 28
after-sales service 60
age 24
aims and objectives 10
authority 40
automation 56
average rate of return (ARR) 74
award schemes 47

B
backwards vertical integration 15
batch production 55
bonus 46
break-even 76
budgets 22
business activity 13
business plan 4

C
cash-flow 78
census statistics 21
chain of command 40
channel 30
climate change 83
communication 42
community 12
companies 9
competitions 28
competitor pricing 27
computers 56
confidence 2
consumer income 84
consumer law 62
cost-plus pricing 27
costs 72
creativity 2
crowd funding 71
Crunch Delight Ltd 88

curriculum vitae (CV) 45
customer 12, 18
  engagement 61
  satisfaction 60
  service 60, 65

D
decision-making 77, 91
decline 26
delegation 40
demand 34
demographic 4
determination 2
digital communication 43
digital distribution 31
direct distribution 30
discrimination 51
disposable income 84
distribution channel 30

E
e-commerce 59
economic climate 84
email 42
employee 12, 47
employment law 51
enterprise 2
entrepreneur 2
environmental considerations 83
ethics 82
external growth 15
external recruitment 44

F
face-to face selling 59
finance 90
  function 68
  sources 70
fixed costs 72
flat structure 41
flexible hours 39
flotation 9
flow production 55
focus group 20

forwards vertical integration 15
free samples 28
fringe benefits 46
full-time 39
funding 69

G
gender 24
globalisation 86
government 12
gross profit 73
gross profit margin 73
growth 10, 14, 26

H
horizontal integration 15
human resources 38, 90

I
income 24
induction training 48
inorganic growth 15
interdependent nature of business 90
internal
  data 21
  growth 14
  recruitment 44
interview 20
introduction 26
investment 7

J
job description 45
job production 55

L
law 51, 62
legislation 10, 62
liability 7, 8
lifestyle 24
limited liability 8
loans 71
location 24

OCR GCSE **Business**

Location 63
logistics 65
loss 72
loss leaders 28
loyalty 60

M

magazines 21
margin of safety 76
market
  data 34
  research 19
  segmentation 24
  share 10, 34
marketing 18
marketing mix 25, 32
maturity 26
merger 15
motivation 46
multinationals (MNCs) 86

N

net profit 73
net profit margin 73
newspapers 21

O

objectives 10
off the job training 49
on the job training 49
operations 90
organic growth 14
organisational structure 39, 40
overdraft 70
owner's capital 71
ownership 6

P

partner 71
partnership 6
part-time 39
pay 46, 51
penetration pricing 27
person specification 45
place 30, 33
planning a business 4
point of sale promotion 28
pollution 83

Porkey's Ltd 36
praise 47
pressure groups 12
price 27, 33
  reductions 28
primary market research 20, 22
print media 29
private limited companies 9
procurement 64
product 25, 33
  knowledge 61
  life cycle 26
production 55, 56
profit 3, 10, 72, 76
  share 46
promotion 28, 33, 35
promotional pricing 27
public limited companies 9

Q

qualitative data 23
quality 58
  assurance 57
  control 57
quantitative data 23
questionnaire 20

R

radio 29
Ravenelli Design Solutions 52
recruitment 44, 51, 69
retailer 30
retained profit 71
retention 46
returns and recalls 58
revenue 72
reward 3, 91
risk 2, 3, 4, 91
robotics 56

S

sales process 61
secondary research 21, 22
segmentation 24
selection 45
self-employed 39
selling 59
selling assets 71

share capital 71
shareholder 12
skimming 27
social media 29, 42
sole trader 6
sources of finance 70
span of control 40
Stabler Gyms 16
staff development 50
stakeholder 12
StreamFlix PLC 80
subordinate 40
suppliers 12, 64
supply chain 65
sustainability 83
SweetDelights Ltd 66

T

takeover 15
tall structure 41
target market 19
technology 10, 56
telesales 59
television 29
total costs 72
trade credit 70
training 48
trialling 20

U

unemployment 85
unlimited liability 8
Urban Trend Ltd 92

V

variable costs 72
vertical integration 15
vocational development 50
voting rights 7

W

waste 58, 83
websites 21, 29
wholesaler 30
workforce needs 38
working from home 39

EXAMINATION TIPS

When you practice exam questions, work out your approximate grade using the following table. This table has been produced using a rounded average of past examination series for this GCSE. Be aware that boundaries vary by a few percentage points either side of those shown.

Grade	9	8	7	6	5	4	3	2	1
Boundary	74%	69%	63%	56%	49%	42%	31%	20%	8%

1. Read all the answers in multiple choice questions before you commit, even if you think the first one you read is the answer. Double check the question to ensure you have interpreted it correctly. Another tip is to disregard the answers that you know are clearly wrong and then assess then ones that remain before making your choice.

2. Read the questions carefully as some students give answers to questions they think are appearing rather than the actual question.

3. In calculation questions, one or two marks may be awarded for workings out, even if the final answer is incorrect. Make sure to show your working in case you make a mistake, and the answer is incorrect. Workings also help you check your own answers at the end of an exam.

4. At least 10% of the total marks for the qualification will reward the use of quantitative skills; make sure you have learned the formulae. You may also be examined in your ability to calculate percentages, percentage changes and averages, so ensure you have practised these.

5. Try to not repeat the question in the first line of your response. It will not score you any marks and simply wastes your time. Avoid losing marks as a result of not finishing the paper.

6. When explaining your points, use clear connectives to show that you are developing the point you have made and not moving onto a separate point. These connectives include; *'thus'*, *'therefore'*, *'this means that'*, *'this leads to'*, *'because'* and *'as a consequence'*. This demonstrates your skills of analysis which are assessed in all longer written questions.

7. Ensure that you include application in answers that are specific about the business in the case study. Many students forget this and throw away easy marks that could be the difference between grades.

8. All questions are marked according to their Assessment Objectives. Each question starts with a command word. Make sure you fully understand what each command word requires you to do. Reading the command words at the start of this book will help you with this.

Good luck!

New titles coming soon!

These guides are everything you need to ace your exams and beam with pride. Each topic is laid out in a beautifully illustrated format that is clear, approachable and as concise and simple as possible.

They have been expertly compiled and edited by subject specialists, highly experienced examiners, industry professionals and a good dollop of scientific research into what makes revision most effective. Past examination questions are essential to good preparation, improving understanding and confidence.

- Hundreds of marks worth of examination style questions
- Answers provided for all questions within the books
- Illustrated topics to improve memory and recall
- Specification references for every topic
- Examination tips and techniques
- Free Python solutions pack (CS Only)

Absolute clarity is the aim.

Explore the series and add to your collection at **www.clearrevise.com**

Available from all good book shops

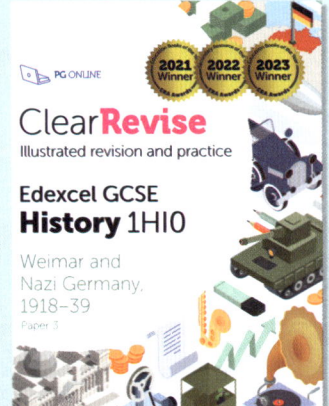

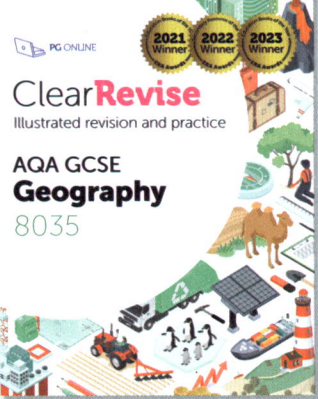

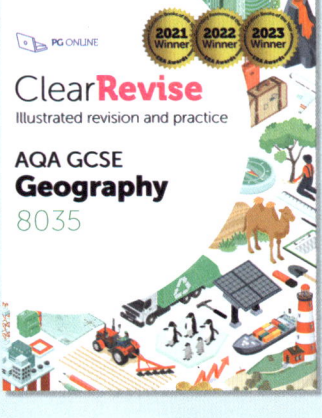

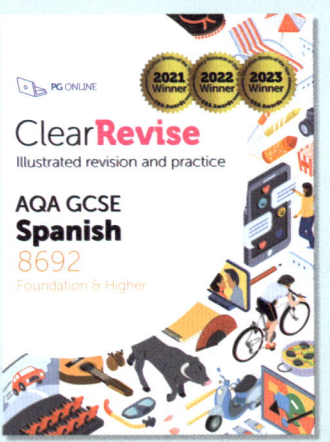

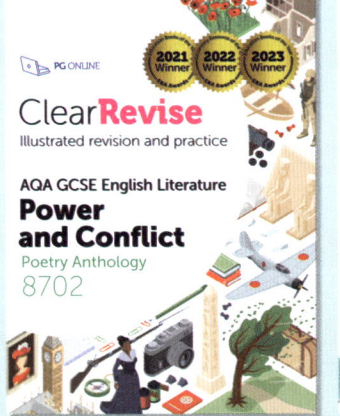

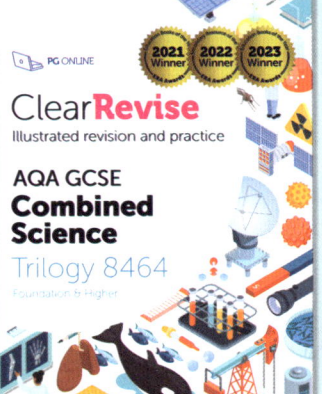

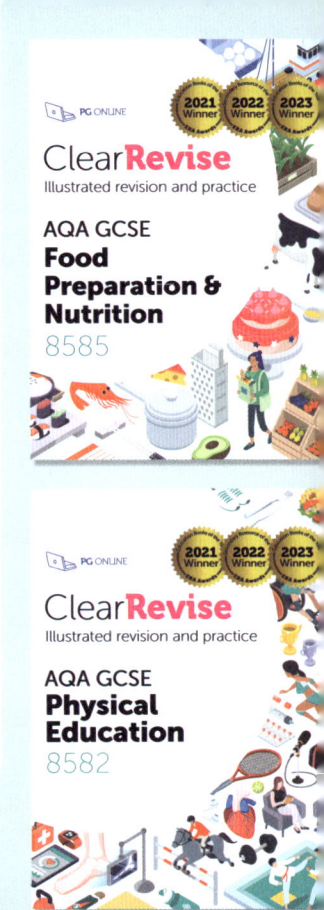

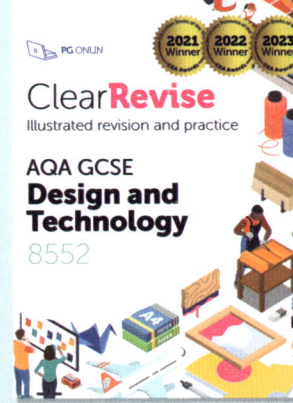

amazon   @pgonlinepub

ClearRevise — Illustrated revision and practice

- AQA GCSE Food Preparation & Nutrition 8585
- AQA GCSE Physical Education 8582
- AQA GCSE English Language 8700
- Edexcel GCSE History 1HI0 — Weimar and Nazi Germany, 1918–39 Paper 3
- AQA GCSE Geography 8035
- OCR GCSE Computer Science J277
- AQA GCSE Spanish 8692 Foundation & Higher
- AQA GCSE English Literature Power and Conflict Poetry Anthology 8702
- AQA GCSE Combined Science Trilogy 8464 Foundation & Higher
- AQA GCSE Design and Technology 8552